AWAKEN YOUR Soul

YOUR ULTIMATE GUIDE TO SPIRITUAL AWAKENING

Lindsay Banks

Awaken Your Soul

© 2020 Lindsay Banks

Cover artwork design by Claire Allen
www.wiltshireartandphotography.co.uk

CONTENTS

I would like to invite you on a journey

Destination: Unknown

Mode of transport: Unknown

Weather: All kinds

Terrain: Rough and smooth

People you may meet: Many and varied

May we journey together with love and compassion

Kindness and empathy

A smile and a laugh

A step forward and backwards

A dance with many

A skip in our step

Following only our hearts and our intuition

Which may guide us on the path

Towards ourselves

Towards a light

Towards love

Embrace the adventure

Embrace the highs and lows

Embrace life

And love

Foreword

When I started writing *A Gentle Hug for the Soul* in 2018, I never imagined I would want to write another book. It surprised me that it took longer to edit and publish the book than actually writing it. To be fair it wasn't a huge book. I hadn't wanted it to be long and complex. I had always envisaged that it would be simple and easy to understand. When I had finished writing it, I thought 'Right, that's it'. I was asked by Dougie Weake from YO1 radio whether there would be a second book, only a month after I had published it. Until then it hadn't crossed my mind. Since then I have realised there is so much more that I need to write about as I take on board the learning for myself. The Universe/Upstairs/Source has kindly gifted me people and experiences since then to further enhance my own spiritual learning and as I work through these and process the information, I apply the new understanding and share these tools with you.

Kindness, Compassion, Empathy, Gratitude, Mindfulness are at the foundation of spirituality. If you consider yourself to practise any of these traits you are spiritual, regardless of any religion or belief system you may affiliate with. As you practise and display these traits you may feel drawn to certain healing modalities or not. If not that's OK. If you do then so your spiritual journey may begin. As we begin to take personal responsibility for our physical bodies, for our emotions, for our mental bodies, we begin to evolve. Understanding ourselves, we begin to evolve. Has your Spiritual Journey begun?

We are all ascending to a new way of living and as we do, it is better to be prepared than not. As I share my journey and my tools it is my wish that you read this and then share with your friends, and family so we all ascend together as a collective.

Acknowledgements

Thank you to my family, friends and loved ones who continue to support me, in my sometimes what seem like crazy endeavours.

Thank you to everyone who I have been so lucky to have met since A Gentle Hug for the Soul was launched. Every interaction I have with another soul brings a new experience, a new perspective. I learn so much more about myself from these interactions.

Thank you to Upstairs/Universe/Source for continuing to guide me and give me the inspirational words that they want to bring to you.

Thank you to Ryan for gifting me some of the biggest lessons that I have had to wade through and learn in order to evolve and grow on my spiritual journey. Patience has been the biggest lesson.

Thank you to everyone who supports me through reading my blog posts, watching my YouTube videos, and recommending my books and resources to others. I truly appreciate you all.

Thank you x

OMNISM

The recognition and respect of all religions and lack thereof. All religion contains truths but not one religion offers all that is truth.

— INTRODUCTION —
THE AWAKENING OF
THE CONSCIOUS

"All the world's a stage,
And all the men and women merely players;
They have their exits and their entrances"
—William Shakespeare, As You Like It

I HAVE NEVER seen or read this play but as I sat during a meditation the words kept rolling around my mind. I asked them to leave but they kept coming back. Sometimes after a meditation I will open my eyes and start writing. For whatever reason I chose to close my eyes and I feel as if the message came through clearer. I always thought these messages came from the Universe/Source/Upstairs or whatever you want to call it. However, I have finally come to the realisation that my channelled messages are coming from a group of higher beings called The Pleidians (I share more about them in the book). I have inadvertently been channelling them for some time without realising it. From the age of 18 when I told a group of classmates we were put here as part of a big experiment to recently telling anyone and everyone who would listen that the word 'should' needed to be eradicated from the dictionary.

I have finally come to accept this fact and I trust what they tell me. It is always loving and guided. My channelling helped me write part of A Gentle Hug for the Soul and has also helped with this book. I feel that more than ever we need spiritual guidance as the world changes and evolves. In this book, I share tools which will help guide you through your own spiritual awakening and onwards on your spiritual journey. Please note that this isn't a set path. We all come across different themes at different times. Whilst one person may be learning about the Divine Masculine and Feminine, someone else may be learning about the Pleiadeans. We can't be experts in every field, which is why I created The Spiritual Journey, a YouTube programme where I speak to experts in their field to create awareness of who is out there and what they do.

Our spiritual path isn't linear and when we feel we have healed one area of our life; this may come up again for us to be healed in another way. It is my hope that these tools bring an awareness to you, so when you come across them on your spiritual path, they won't shock you.

Here is a piece I channelled, which I feel lends some explanation for the craziness which was going on in the world in 2019

28/7/2019

I went to a Chinese restaurant
To buy a loaf of bread. bread, bread
He wrapped it up in a five pound note a
And this is what he said, said, said

My name is Eli Eli
Chickali Chickali
Roli Poli

(This was the start of a clapping song I used to sing as a child)
I was then given this to share

Nonsensical. Songs. We sing songs that make no sense. Yet when we live in a nonsensical world, we try to make sense of it. We try to apply logic and reason. It doesn't work. The world is changing so you can see it for what it really is. It has become disturbing and a farce. The curtains will fall. Like at the end of a play. The actors will disappear behind them and all that will be left is the audience, the observers, the seers. You will be left wondering where they have gone. They have fulfilled their duty and purpose. Now it is time for you to rise up to yours.

When all the actors on the stage have left with their dramas and stories. What are you left with? A sense of awe and wonder? Or a sense of disappointment? What can I do now? You wonder? Where am I? or who am I without the drama, the excitement and those I have been merely watching. Tune inwards and find your inner frequency. Where is it?

I never know what I am going to write or what subject we are writing about. I act merely as the channel. I didn't want to be a channeller or conduit. I told upstairs I didn't want to be the one speaking to higher beings and talking about it. But you know what? This is me. I channel. I know, in my heart, I need to share these channelled writings with you. This book has a combination of my channelled writing and my own learning and observations since continuing along my spiritual journey. My hope is that it helps you with your own spiritual awakening.

The energies are shifting, the patriarchal system that we have known for so long is collapsing. The tide is turning. Our lives, as we have known them are changing. Your perception of what is possible is changing. You are becoming aware of all that is around you. You are awakening.

— 1 —
AWAKENING
& DIMENSIONS

AWAKENINGS ARE OCCURRING across the globe on a daily basis irrelevant of sex, gender, race or religion. It isn't something we can 'control' We decided before we came to Earth that we wanted to be born in this time, a time of ascension, a time of real spiritual growth. However, what I am finding is that when the awakenings are occurring people are feeling lost, not sure who to turn to. They may be turning their back on faith and belief systems which have always been in place for them. A steady structure on which to rely on. You may have had the same job for 30 years and then get made redundant. Your marriage may have collapsed. You may have lost someone close to you. Spiritual awakenings often occur following a loss or tragedy in someone's life. You start to question Why am I here? What is my life purpose? What does all of this mean? You start to ask yourself whether working 9–5 is what life is about.

An advert for Gaia TV keeps popping up. It says, *"People all over the planet are waking up"* Towards the end of 2018 I kept telling people how 2019 was going to be an exciting year, not just for me but for everyone. There has been a huge shift in energies so far. Time seems to have speeded up. Many people that I know have been going through karmic release. Letting go of 'stuff' that no longer serves them. Turns out 2020 is seeing a huge shake up for many too.

Even if you don't class yourself as spiritual, reading this section can prepare you for what some people call "The Dark night of the Soul". I am sure that some people are misdiagnosed when they go to see a GP, or talking to their friends and family. Those closest to you might think you have gone crazy. Or there is something wrong with you. Awakening symptoms can be similar to signs of depression, as you'll see from my own and others' stories here.

The first time I heard the words 'Awakening' and 'Fifth Dimension' was from one of my Reiki students. I'd never heard the terms before and wasn't really sure what they were. Two months later another student came to me telling me about her awakening. I started to read into it so I could understand it if more clients or students came to me, which they did. Fast forward a couple of years and now I get it! Let me explain first of all what an awakening is and then I can describe the dimensions of consciousness.

Urban Dictionary describes it as *a shift in consciousness, an apperception of reality which had been previously unrealized. The culmination of such realizations is in the recognition of oneness with all of existence."* My more simplified version would be, "*Remembering who you truly are".*

What does that mean? 'I AM ME.' Yes, you are. However, you were born and brought up within a family, or not, who had certain beliefs and thoughts. Their beliefs and thoughts unconsciously will have become your beliefs and thoughts.

You went to school and the teachers gave you knowledge and opinions which you unconsciously absorbed. You left school and may have got your first job. You were working for someone who had their own ways and ideas of working, which you adopted. They had their set of beliefs and opinions which you unconsciously absorbed. You may get tired of working 9–5 and doing the same thing every day. You arrive home feeling tired and exhausted. Thinking to yourself that there must be more to life than this. This is the beginning of the process. You may start watching Gaia as you are intrigued. You may search YouTube videos searching for proof that you are meant to be here, that there is something higher at work. You may start to read self-help books and you may start to question who you are. Maybe you start hearing about higher beings, multi dimensions, healing, shamans, auras, angels. Some of the stuff you hear or read or watch might blow your mind. It might feel so far out of your minds current capability that you struggle to absorb any of it or take it in.

My own mind has been BLOWN learning about even more about myself and life than I knew or thought possible. After publishing *A Gentle Hug for the Soul* in 2018, I thought that was it. I had grown, expanded and learnt so much there couldn't be much more could there? How wrong was I and how egoic! I want to share my own experience of awakening so you can compare it with your own, or recognise when it happens to you in the future.

WHAT HAPPENS WHEN YOU START TO AWAKEN?

Once you start to awaken, you're on a path – there's no going back. For some people an awakening can happen quite quickly, which can make it seem quite scary. For others it is more of a gradual journey. I liken my awakening to that of the

Tortoise in the Tortoise and the Hare. It started back in 2002 when I first heard about Reiki. Since then I have experienced different healing, read hundreds of books, watched thousands of YouTube videos and Gaia programmes. I meditate to develop myself, I practise Yoga, most days. I work on myself every day so I can be in the best place to help others. I have had the time to be able to observe various tools and gained a broad understanding of this journey.

There are five stages with spiritual awakening that I have identified, and not everybody's is the same. Some people's awakenings occur post tragedy or trauma. The loss of a loved one, a divorce, a nasty accident. You are left thinking what is life about? What is the meaning of life? Why am I here? What's my purpose? You start digging for meaning. These stages are based on my experience and those of my clients.

STAGE 1

This is probably the most confusing time. You have no idea what the hell is going on. You've never heard of an awakening. You just know you don't feel quite right and things don't sit with you as well as they did. Signs of an awakening may include

- Starting to question who you are and why you behave in certain ways. You start to look beyond you as a physical being and start to reflect on your behaviours.

- Beginning to remove judgement and opinions of others based on their appearance, status, car they drive. Becoming aware that they are human too

- Questioning your belief system. Are the beliefs you currently hold yours? Or have they been instilled in you from your parents? Your family?

- A willingness to be open minded and becoming aware of synchronicities happening around you

- You may find you are becoming more compassionate and can empathise with others more easily due to situations or experiences that you have had.

- You have no fear of death as you begin to live mindfully and in the present. You see death as part of the process of life

- You may find yourself unable to sleep or waking at the same time every morning

- Some people report having headaches and migraines

- You may experience ringing in your ears. This can be a sign of angels, downloads and your body becoming attuned to a higher vibration

- You may find yourself becoming extra sensitive to large crowds and noise as you are open to others energies

- You may feel a desire to connect with nature more, to be outside, to walk in forests or woods and really connect with the earth

- You start to eat healthier foods and desire to look after your physical body

- Your vision may become blurry and you may start to see things that you couldn't before. You may see sparkles of green or purple light, white outlines around people or you may see objects in your peripheral vision.

- You may experience flu like symptoms. I recently felt like this and asked what was up. I was told Ascension flu. This is where your physical body is catching up with the spiritual and emotional healing changes you have gone through

These are some of the signs that you may experience. If you are in physical or emotional pain do seek help from a doctor or trained professional in their field. A spiritual awakening isn't easy but it is rewarding.

STAGE 2

This is when the realisation hits that you need to get out of this hole you are currently in. How do you do that? By finding other people who have been in it, by talking to them. By beginning to practise meditation, healing, yoga, journaling. Start to listen to what your soul wants you to know. What passions do you have that you would like to pursue? Is there a destination that you have maybe always wanted to visit? Start making changes to your daily life.

STAGE 3

This stage is acceptance. You are mastering the art of practising various tools that are keeping you on track, mentally. Emotionally you still may have up and down days. These will always be with you as you start to adapt to the rhythms of natural life, not the work life you may have been conditioned to. You accept that you are on a different path to the one you maybe thought you were going down

STAGE 4

This is when you have worked on yourself and feel in a good place. You then can share your own awakening story with someone else who maybe needs to hear it

STAGE 5

This is the realisation that this is just the beginning. Like an onion, as you heal, there is more to be healed, more to be learned. The spiritual journey is an exciting one, if you allow it to be. As well as having its more challenging moments. It is how we choose to respond and how much we are willing to heal ourselves in order to heal others, in order to heal our children and our planet.

Another thing to be aware of during the awakening process is that, as we begin to ascend through dimensions, we may get what is known as Ascension Flu. As we move towards becoming lighter beings and into the next dimension many of us may be feeling 'out of sorts' and maybe not knowing why.

WHAT IS ASCENSION FLU?

I need to explain firstly what happened in the days leading up to me finding out what 'Ascension Flu' is. It started with a fall. I fell over and hurt myself. A lot. Initially, I couldn't walk on my ankle. I went to the GP who said I may have broken it. I then drove myself to hospital on a Friday afternoon at 5pm only to be told there was a 3.5hour wait. I had literally thrown my kids into my neighbour's house and couldn't hang around. Anyway, if they put a plaster cast on me, how would I get home? I cried to the receptionist that I couldn't stay and would head home. I drove home and asked in my Facebook group for some healing to be sent to my ankle. The next morning, I woke up and the pain had subsided, a lot. I headed to London and was able to walk on it. The following week my shoulder started hurting and I could barely lift my arm. In my head I asked what was wrong with me. Internal rotator cuff, I was told. OK, who do I need to see about this? Physio I was told again. I didn't go to the doctor instead I went straight to a physio and had several sessions. I hate being in pain, so just wanted to get it sorted. Following that I kept getting stomach pain, then waves of nausea would hit at unexpected times. I woke up at 130am two nights in a row.

The first night I woke up and channelled stuff about politics, the upcoming election in December 2019 and the NHS. I felt as if I was on the cusp of something big.

"This last week I have felt strange. I have experienced what I can only describe as hot flashes through my body. Literally feeling as if my body is on fire for no reason. My eyes have been blurry. I have been waking up at 1 or 2 in the morning for no reason. I have felt compelled to write about politics and the NHS, not my bag really, but this is what I have channelled. I have felt 'out of place' whilst being in the world. I have wanted to be by myself, most of the time in solitude. I have had a massive creative outburst."

The physical symptoms started about two weeks prior to the above entry. I had this feeling in my solar plexus area, in my stomach that felt like a knot. No amount of Reiki, healing or meditating could shift it. I tried ecstatic dance, which worked for a couple of days and 5rhythms.

I remember taking myself out for a walk and asking upstairs, why am I feeling out of sorts? I was given the term Ascension Flu in my mind. What on earth is that? I thought. Is that even a thing? I asked on Twitter but there was only tumbleweed.

I turned to my trusty google to find out if anyone else had experienced this and I found a few articles online. A lot of this now makes sense! Ascension sickness occurs when our bodies are changing their physical structure. This may sound a little bit crazy but our bodies are moving from being a carbon copy to crystalline.

The fact that there has been such a rise in veganism and plant-based diets is indicative of the fact that our tastes are changing and will continue to do so. We aren't only eating less animals because of our tastes but because we are recognising at a conscious level that eating animals and meat doesn't serve us. We don't technically need it, although scientists may argue we do for iron. Spinach is a great substitute for this. I'm not a nutritionist. I only write what I am given/ told. As we continue to evolve spiritually, we begin to make changes to our diet, to our environment, to our relationships, it therefore stands to reason that things are going to change within too and in our energetic systems. As we meditate and begin to work on clearing and raising our vibration, we are going to face challenges which will grow and test us. As we do and face these in a different way, as we have learnt, we grow more. Healing works on so many different levels and it is like an onion. Once you start peeling back the layers there is more to work on. I joke with my students that once you think right that's it, my healing work is complete, boom, along comes something else. It may be a particular area of your life. Control has been a recent one of mine. Where am I trying to control my life? What can I let go of? What aspects of my life don't I need to control? How can I trust even more that the Universe has my back? Once we have healed our own personal traumas, we may do ancestral healing, and then carry on and on, healing all the hurts we have ever felt and bringing them to the surface to be healed. I am not going to lie this can feel physically painful. I have sobbed driving home, for what felt like no reason, but feeling extreme discomfort in my solar plexus area. It feels uncomfortable. I kept being advised to breathe into it. I did. Sometimes it helped and sometimes I just had to cry. If I didn't know what I know I would have thought that I was going through a nervous breakdown. Literally having no control over my feelings, thinking I was hallucinating one night. I do wonder whether there are misdiagnoses happening across the globe, as people may be experiencing these awakenings and symptoms without realising it.

WHAT ARE THE SYMPTOMS?

Ascension flu occurs when our physical bodies fail to keep up with our spiritual growth. We are aligning with energies and frequencies which may not have been felt before. As we head through 2020 and beyond, we are entering a new phase of being and that can affect us physically. We may not feel well, but not really sure why. We may go to the doctors; they may run tests and nothing. It is as if you have the actual 'flu' but different. Below are some of the symptoms.

- Dizziness

- Nausea

- Pains and aches within the body that can't be explained by a doctor

- Hot flashes through the body

- Waking up through the night and not being able to go back to sleep, or if you do only for a couple of hours

- Extremely vivid dreams

- A change in diet

- Headaches- Our 3rd eye chakra and pineal gland may be opening, allowing us to connect to ourselves and the other side.

- Sore throat- For many of us we have kept quiet about the work we do and maybe even our beliefs, hiding them from friends and family. Our throat chakra is the place where we communicate from. As our energies ascend, we are more likely to share these beliefs with others.

- Ringing in ears- this is opening up our clairaudience.

- Sensitivity to noise

- Cravings for particular types of foods. I haven't eaten nachos in years then had them twice in one week! Eat what your body wants you to eat. Some of us may comfort eat at this time as we want to protect our solar plexus area

- Crying for no reason. I have never cried as much as I have the last 4–6 weeks. Sobbing my heart out at the wheel of my car whilst singing to Ellie Goulding.
- Gritty or blurry eyes
- Skin issues

I would always recommend getting checked over if you do feel out of sorts but having this awareness can help you when going through a spiritual growth period.

How can you get through Ascension flu?

The biggest tip I would say is to be kind to yourself. If you have a daily routine of meditating or yoga carry on. If not, you might want to think about how you can implement these into your life. Take nana naps if you can. Even a ten-minute snooze in the car before you pick your kids up from school can help. Go to bed early. Eat what you feel like eating. Ask your body, is this what my body needs right now? Allow yourself to go with the flow. The benefit of ascension flu is that once this has passed you will be more aligned energetically, and this will cause a ripple effect to your family and friends and loved ones around you.

Part of your awakening is about remembering your inner purpose. When you are going through an awakening you will have a lot of questions. Relationships will change. You will find that toxic or negative people fall by the wayside. You may find yourself coming into conflict with your nearest and dearest as they don't want to hear certain 'truths'. The reason your relationships change is that as you awaken or begin to heal yourself your vibration changes. The people who were around you before are still the same – their vibration may not be changing at the same time as yours. People whose energy no longer resonates with yours may get annoyed or angry with you. I remember being told that I had changed a lot in 7 years. Yes, I thought. If I hadn't changed in 7 years I would be gutted! Healing and transformation go hand in hand. As you heal you wake up to the real you. Some of your beliefs may not sit well with others. They won't like it. Maybe you no longer agree with that person's beliefs and no matter how hard you try the relationship is just not flowing anymore. If you try to fight and resist and cling onto a relationship that is no longer working for you it can result in hurt and emotional pain. Let it go. Singing the Frozen song really helps with reaffirming this message to ourselves.

Coming into the moment and experiencing mindfulness reminds us to spend each day being fully present. When we have that mindful awareness relationships can become much easier. You think about where you are right now, not in ten or twenty years – you loosen your attachment to the past or the future.

One way or another, as you awaken your relationships will change. Of that I am certain. As long as you have that awareness also you can be prepared for that. You may feel completely alone. You may be used to being surrounded by people. Learning to be comfortable in and with solitude is a big lesson and one that can be helpful to you on your spiritual journey – you tune into yourself more rather than look to what others are doing.

PRACTICAL TIPS

If you are feeling alone, do reach out. There are LOADS of online groups you can become a member of where there are people to talk to who may have been through the same situation as you and can share their thoughts. My Facebook group, Consciousness Arising, is a safe, online community where people can openly ask questions on awakening, dreams, synchronicities

http://www.facebook.com/groups/ConsciousnessArising

If you find groups near you, maybe yoga, meditation, women's circles, men's circles, you will find your own tribe of people who you can connect with. The spiritual journey can mean that you will actively seek time alone as you learn to deal with others energies. When you have your alone time, meditate, bathe in salt water, practise yoga, journal.

You might find your diet changing. Some of my students have said they have literally woken up one day and decided not to eat meat anymore. I have been a meat eater for years and in August 2019 I decided I didn't want to eat meat anymore and I'm quite enjoying it. I feel lighter in my body. There is a huge shift to plant-based diets and veganism. You don't have to be Vegan to be spiritual. My dad made me laugh, when I told him I didn't eat meat anymore he sat there for about 5 minutes, then looked at me. "What do you eat then?" he asked. Vegetables and beans, I told him. He shook his head and laughed.

I read recently that an awakening into ascension is a bit like puberty. The puberty stage is well researched and talked about. Everyone knows that when a child hits 11/12 it's a new beginning for them. It can happen a bit later for some and a bit earlier for others but there is a definite time span for it.

The same can't be said for a spiritual awakening. As there is no set age that it happens I think it can be more difficult for people to understand. We have the term 'midlife crisis'. When I was younger, I thought that was 40, now as I approach 40, I feel it is 50. When people start to approach what they see as halfway through their life and think, what am I doing with my life? I need to ride a motorbike, buy a flash car, head off to India for a month, whatever it looks like for that person. Or a tragedy may trigger an awakening. A death in the family. A divorce. Something unexpected that alters and shifts your perception from this time and space. It rocks your world. It makes you wonder, is this all there is? And you realise there is more. This is where the awakening begins.

Awakening can feel like a lonely, isolating experience as we acclimatise to our new way of being. I had no idea what was going on for me during my own awakening as I had no awareness of what it was. Even though I had read books, attended workshops and meditated no one had ever mentioned the term, "spiritual awakening". It is only looking back that I realised what had happened. My own awakening occurred following the passing of my friend, Lisa and then going through a divorce several months later. Lisa's passing was my trigger. I sobbed with grief and I realised I had become emotionally numb to life. Every day was like Groundhog Day. I would get up, look after my kids, go out, come home, speak to my husband, have dinner, watch TV and go to bed. Then do it all again the next day. I didn't realise that I wasn't allowing myself to feel any extremes of emotions until Lisa passed away. Allowing myself to grieve and feel such strong emotions was a shock. I wasn't used to this. Crying. I couldn't remember the last time I had properly sobbed and let 'stuff' out. Several months later my husband and I decided to divorce. We were both advised to live together for six months. To say they were a difficult six months would be an understatement. This was my beginning; my spiritual awakening had begun.

I wanted to share someone else's story with you so you can see how everyone's experience of a spiritual awakening is unique. My friend, Lizi Walker, has kindly agreed to share her story of her own awakening here.

LIZI'S STORY

I was in a relationship with someone for around 5 years who was emotionally and psychologically abusing me, to the point it caused complex post-traumatic stress disorder. The shock of realising this person had set out to destroy me from day one is what set off my awakening - a journey of self-discovery, healing and truth. I had no idea these types of people even existed, people without a conscience. I was extremely traumatised at this point; I was unable to trust anybody or let anyone in. I was so weak and tired I spent weeks at a time in bed not eating or having the strength to get out, I was in an extremely dark and lonely place. I felt like I'd been touched by the devil. My hair fell out at one side, thick chunks of skin all over my hands was dying and peeling off, I had water infections, I lost lots of weight and aged around 10 years, just walking up and down stairs left me feeling the need to sleep. I actually thought I was dying. I was hearing voices, jumping at my own shadow, so I spent most of my time in my bedroom. That had become my safe place, with 2 locks on the door and CCTV, that's how scared and paranoid I'd become, not knowing who anyone was any more or who I could trust. I thought I was going crazy and everyone was out to hurt me. The pain of the past came creeping in, I felt like I was being dragged back to all the things I'd buried away and never healed or dealt with. At this point I was on my hands and knees screaming, crying, begging God to help me, asking what I done so wrong to deserve this pain. I'd never really believed in God or anything else but at this point I felt I had to believe in something, something I didn't even know existed as it was all I had. This went on for quite some time and I spent over a year battling this on my own, feeling isolated and alone, as anybody I did speak to about it looked at me like I was crazy. I certainly felt crazy, I was hearing people whispering my name in the garden, seeing the ghost of a little boy in my bathroom. Voices in my head which, I knew I wasn't putting there. During this time, I felt like I was being guided by something or someone I couldn't see, but it was all I had so I had to let go and trust it. Because hanging on and fighting was just prolonging the pain and suffering. Then an old friend got in touch and saw what I was going through and sent me a video, 10 signs you're going through a spiritual awakening. I watched the video while shaking and crying as I resonated with every single word on it now my mind was totally blown . . . what the hell was going on? I remember saying to my doctor "you couldn't make this stuff up what's happening to me" I felt like I was tripping, none of it felt real. It was like I was experiencing this whole different world that no one else could see. The friend that sent me the video started to come round and she showed me how to ground myself, we'd go over the riverbank across from my house and take our shoes off and push all the negativity out into mother earth and give thanks for everything we were grateful for that day. She also introduced me to crystals, I remember thinking yeah right this is just a stone. She told me to hold the crystal in the sun and it sent a shock up my arm I was like WOW this really isn't just a stone; she gave me a piece of rose quartz for self-love and told me to keep it with me. This was a massive help to me, slowly I started getting better days. A glimpse of hope that maybe there was a sign of light in this extremely dark place I'd found myself in. I'd read on a psychopath free site I was on, that if you manage to survive the psychopathic experience what you would receive at the end would be so worth it. I struggled to see this, still having several extremely dark days at a time. Then a lady called Sharon from my local mind charity got in touch, offering to help me. At this point I'd saved up lots of medication, I'd planned to take my own life. I was tired of fighting on my own. I was such a negative thinker I had been on antidepressants for anxiety for 21 years, I tried to get help, my doctor told me that he didn't think we could change my way of thinking, I'd thought like it for too long. I walked out of there thinking, 'watch me'. I managed to hold on until the following week, when Sharon came. She listened to me without judging and validated that what I'd gone through was real, from this point everything started to change. Sharon came to see me every week, I'd decided I could do this, I came off medication and I started meditating. I put positive affirmations beside my bed which I would say every morning, things like " I am lovable", "I can achieve anything I put my mind to", "amazing things are going to happen to me today", I started telling myself I was beautiful and that I loved myself, even though I didn't believe it I just kept saying it until I did. During this time, I found Reiki, I would do a morning Reiki meditation, I'd found on YouTube, as soon as I woke up to help set my day off on a positive note. I was so afraid of going back to that dark place I decided I had to push myself to do things I'd never dared to do before. I started to get a new lease of life; I'd finally started to see things differently. I started to love myself and believe in myself, I realised I was so much more than I'd been led to believe. So, I decided I'd jump on a plane to Marrakesh on my own to volunteer for a week with disadvantaged kids. Then I decided I needed to give something back to my local mind charity and I jumped out of a plane at 10,000 ft and did two radio interviews about it and raised a thousand pounds for them just to say thank you. I was now on this massive high I was bouncing through life I actually cried tears of happiness on several occasions I couldn't believe I could feel such immense happiness from just being alive and not taking any kind of drug. Everything suddenly looked beautiful I would just sit in a field and buzz of the amazing view. I would drive round chasing a view of the sunsets in total awe of it. I can't even begin to describe how amazing I felt and I started to manifest amazing things into my reality at the drop of a hat. It was mind blowing. I am now extremely grateful to my ex, he may have destroyed me but he only destroyed the fake me, the me I'd built up around myself to protect myself. The journey he took me on was one of stripping away the old to rebirth the real me, the true me and to learn to love myself, forgive myself and always believe in myself. He awoke me to the truths that ripped me apart, but truths that also built me and helped me make me who I am today. I've now been off prescription drugs for 2 and a half years and I've never felt better, I've passed my Reiki level 1 and level 2, with Lindsay as my teacher. I've got my Indian head massage diploma and I've just started my shamanic practitioners' course. I now know what I went through was a Dark Night of the Soul and a kundalini awakening."

Lizi's story is just one of many stories that I hear regarding spiritual awakening. It was through Lizi, that I actually first heard of the term. I am happy to report that Lizi is now helping others also on their spiritual journey through Reiki healing and other healing modalities.

WHAT IS A DARK NIGHT OF THE SOUL?

Now that you have an awareness of spiritual awakening, I want to bring your attention to a term that is often used in terms of our awakening.

It sounds quite ominous. The term comes from a poem written in the 1500's by St John of the Cross. He describes it as 'the method followed by the soul in its journey upon the spiritual road to the attainment of the perfect union with God" Personally I would substitute the word God, with Source, the Universe, but use a word you feel comfortable with. It doesn't occur generally in one night. For some people this last days, weeks, months. The sooner we recognise what we are going through the sooner we can start to put tools into place to come through it slightly easier. The Dark Night of the Soul often occurs following a traumatic event. Maybe the loss of a loved one, a car crash, divorce, a major accident or period of illness.

In Lizi's case it was her ex-partner. For me, it was losing Lisa to cancer on my 36th birthday. I hadn't realised up until that point how emotionally numb I had become to everything around me. My Dark Night of the Soul came during the six months afterwards. The realisation that life wasn't about material goods. The realisation that everything I had built up in my own life was now falling apart. The breaking down of the family unit. All of the structures and routines that I had built up to keep myself safe and protected came crashing down around me.

How might you be feeling during your Dark Night of the Soul?

- Lost

- Stuck

- Confused

- Feeling sadness for yourself and the world around you

- A feeling of hopelessness and powerlessness

- Lacking interest in things you used to enjoy

- A sense of melancholy

- Feeling disconnected to life

When we experience our Dark Night of the Soul it can feel like it is going on forever. It occurs so we can become who we were born to be. To remember why we are here. I would love to tell you that this may only happen once in your lifetime and you're done. Unfortunately, I can't. I had this belief and then went through another one in 2019. Shedding even more 'stuff' and healing not only myself, but ancestral and karmic lines. I would also love to say it was easier second time around but it wasn't. If anything, it was more challenging. However, I came through it, again. As will you.

One of the tools which helped me massively during this time was meditation. I had tried to meditate years earlier when I worked in retail. I remember sitting on the edge of my bed, reading a book, How to Meditate in 5 easy steps and throwing it across my bedroom. I could not quiet my mind. I couldn't still my mind. This was ridiculous. I meditated on and off using guided meditations over the years but didn't practise it consistently. During my Dark Night of the Soul I felt I needed to meditate. I would listen to a guided meditation by Tony Stockwell called How to Meet Your Spirit

Guide. I wanted to connect with my spirit guide, as I had been told they can guide you through certain situations in life. I was aware of who my spirit guides were but I had never made contact. After six weeks of listening to this meditation my Spirit Guide appeared in my mind's eye. He was a native American Indian. Why am I here? I asked him. "To teach, to educate and inform" To teach what I asked him? He laughed and disappeared. I found meditating extremely helpful in terms of quietening my mind, becoming more mindful and calming in a period of chaos. I started using Reiki again on myself to self-heal and again to bring those calming energies in. I would lie in bed at night asking which of my chakras were out of balance and place crystals on them. I visited the Spiritualist church, nearly weekly, to see if mediums could confirm that I was doing the right thing and they did. I started getting to know me again. I used a combination of affirmations, gratitude, mindfulness. I spoke to the Angels and asked for help. There were nights that I would go to bed and cry myself to sleep. I asked the angels once for a hug and felt this huge embrace around me. I dreamt that Archangel Michael came in and cut the cords for me between myself and my ex. When I woke up in the morning, I said thank you.

Awakenings and Dark Nights of the Soul are different for everyone. If you have been through one yourself, I would love to hear your story. If you haven't then please keep reading as you will find some tools in here to support you and navigate you on your journey. Having that awareness of what an awakening is before you get to it can make it a lot less scary and knowing there are others out there who have gone through it and come out the other side, also makes it a lot less scary.

Please remember if you haven't yet experienced your own Dark Night of the Soul, that when it comes, if it comes, there is a light at the end of the tunnel. When you come through it, there will be many transformations that have taken place, inwardly, which will then create external changes in your life.

PRACTICAL TIPS FOR GETTING THROUGH THE DARK NIGHT OF THE SOUL

- Be kind to yourself. This is a transformative journey you are undertaking

- Meditate

- Journal

- Seek healing

- Practise yoga, mindfulness, gratitude

- Connect with nature

- Fresh air

- Eating healthy foods

- Sleeping when you need to

When you have come through your Dark Night of the Soul where are you actually headed? What is next? If you are going through your own Dark Night of the Soul do share it with others #Awakenyoursoul. The more of us who understand it and are aware of it, the more support we can get for it.

Let's go into dimensions of consciousness so it might make more sense.

There are currently 12 states of dimensional consciousness. The main ones currently on Earth are 3D, 4D and 5D. Depending on which dimension we are living in will depend on how we perceive the world. Let me give you some examples so you can see where you are right now

3D Consciousness

- You view things as physical, rather than energy and vibration

- Life is a competition and people are judged by the way they dress, the car they drive, the smartphone they have

- Things are perceived as good or bad, right or wrong

- You don't believe that thoughts can change your reality. If something happens it is a coincidence

- Money and social status are high priority

- You have no desire to go within yourself and look at things from a higher point of view

- You don't believe there is enough for everyone in the world: money, food etc

We have been very much ensconced in the 3D world for a very long time. Pre-Dark Night of the Soul and awakening this is where you may be at. As you enter your Dark Night you veer into 4D Consciousness

4D Consciousness

- Seen as a path to the 5th Dimension

- You might change your eating habits, start to meditate, do some yoga

- You have started to believe that there is something more than 'just this'

- You start to think about your impact on the environment, reducing plastic, recycling, using the car less

- You want to find your purpose and follow your dreams

- Your intuition starts to grow and expand

- You are looking for a deeper meaning to life and the Universe

This is a process. Some people in the spiritual world call this 'upleveling' where you are moving from level to the next. I often refer to the 4D as No Man's Land. It is a difficult space to be in as you hover between the 3D and 5D however you can get through it.

5D CONSCIOUSNESS

- Once you are here it is very difficult to go back to 3D life
- You understand the connection and oneness of life
- There is no good or bad when an event occurs, it just is
- You understand that there is a higher purpose at work
- You have stronger feelings of love connection, with others, with the Earth, the Moon, the Stars,
- There is no judgement of others, they walk their path in their way, you do it your way
- You see everyone as equal, regardless of their social status in the world
- Your purpose in life is to live in joy and truth
- No competition and enough for everyone
- Your intuition is very strong

Those are your 3 levels of consciousness and you are exactly where you need to be right now. Everyone's path is different. Everyone's journey is unique. Embrace the journey for whilst some may amble through from the 3rd to the 5th, others may find themselves catapulted into the 5th overnight.

My own awakening has been slow and steady. Because of that it has made it much easier to deal with when things have come up for me. A couple of my Reiki students had much more sudden awakenings. Everyone has different awakenings and there isn't a one size fits all when it comes to having one.

A great phrase my friend says is, "This Too Shall Pass." When you start to awaken trust that it is the beginning of a process. You are shedding crap that no longer serves you and isn't going to serve you. Yes, it can be frightening if you have always lived according to someone else's beliefs and opinions. TRUST in the process.

— 2 —
MEDITATION

I FIRST SAT down to meditate ten years ago after buying myself a book called Teach yourself to Meditate. I remember reading it then sitting down on the edge of my bed to quiet my mind. After two minutes I gave up and threw the book across the room. How was I meant to quiet my mind? I was a manager in a large retail store and would often work twelve-hour days. My mind was full of work stuff, me stuff, emotional stuff. There was no way I could do this.

I dabbled in and out of meditating for a few years when I would go to spiritual workshops. It wasn't until I faced my own challenging time that I realised the importance of meditating. I only had one meditation CD in the house. YouTube wasn't that big then, or maybe it was but I wasn't aware of it. After my friend passed and I was going through the grieving process I wanted something to distract my mind. I still hadn't learnt the art of stilling my mind so wanted to listen to what is called a guided meditation. This is where you listen to a person talking, sometimes with background music, sometimes not and they talk you into a deep state of relaxation and then clear your chakras, meet a spirit guide or whatever purpose you choose to meditate. For me, I wanted to meet my spirit guide. I wanted to know that there was an external influence or helper in my life to get me through the grief. I was also getting divorced so had a lot on my mind, as you can imagine.

Initially I found it difficult as I wasn't used to spending time by myself. Gradually it became easier and it allowed my mind to be focused on just listening to Tony Stockwell's voice for forty-five minutes. I couldn't think about my feelings, of sadness, of guilt, of loss. This was my time. A time of no distractions, of focusing on my breath, of clearing my mind, of being present and not worrying about what could happen or what had happened in my past. It was mindful and it helped me stay calm. When I learnt Access Bars and had a treatment my mind finally, finally became clearer. It was much easier to sit in silence and appreciate it. I have two small children so silence isn't something that is easy to come by in my house. When we put down our digital devices and spend time breathing and by ourselves it not only brings calm and stillness but it can help bring focus and clarity.

How to Meditate

Just making a start is progress. There are a variety of meditation tools available now which can help. If you look on YouTube there are tons of guided meditations and you might feel overwhelmed. Listen to a few just to see whose voice you like; which ones feel calming for you. You can download the Headspace app on your phone. I have personally never used this but have heard great things about it. Or if you want to begin with silent meditation start slowly and build yourself up. Meditation is a practise. Spend 5 minutes with your eyes closed just breathing in and out and focusing on your breath. Switch off all distractions, TV, tablets, mobile phones etc. You can do this at home, in the garden, when you are out walking. If you are wearing sunglasses you can sit with your eyes closed on a bench and no-one will notice. Sometimes, if I have five minutes before I pick the kids up from school, I close my eyes and just focus on my breath.

The more you spend time out meditating the calmer you will start to feel. Meditation has many benefits including reduced anxiety, gaining clarity, feeling more focused, more present, better sleep. I wish you every success in your meditating journey. Namaste.

— 3 —

THE SHADOW SELF -
BEHIND THE LIGHT
THERE IS DARKNESS

I TAUGHT LEANNE Reiki in the summer of 2018. For a few days afterwards I went on what I can only describe as a downer. I felt awful. I didn't want to do anything. I couldn't stop crying. I didn't feel like me. When I mentioned it to her, she said, "Ah yes that's because I sometimes trigger peoples shadow selves." I just went "ah, I see." But I didn't. I woke up 3 days later back to my usual self and forgot about it.

At the beginning of January 2019, I decided I wanted to do a podcast. Everyone else was doing them so why not me? I conducted an interview with Leanne. Two days later I went on another downer. This time though I remembered what Leanne had said. I had been feeling frustrated and low on energy. I decided to do a bit more research on the 'shadow' and what it means.

WHERE DOES THE SHADOW COME FROM?

Carl Jung, physician and psychiatrist, described the shadow as 'that hidden, repressed, inferior and guilt laden personality'. The shadow is a part of us that we can't avoid. True spirituality can come from the expression or integration of the shadow. It requires us to consciously accept and relate to our shadow. When we repress, project, act out and remain unconscious of it, we struggle to grow.

"Without the conscious inclusion of the shadow in daily life there can't be an individual relationship to the divine. (Dr Diamond, Psychology Today) The shadow can be seen as those parts of you that maybe aren't seen as 'acceptable' in society. Traits such as anger, impatience, laziness, greed. It is what you perceive to be dark and weak about yourself and therefore needs to be hidden and denied. We are conditioned to hide these traits from an early age. Having tantrums isn't seen as being acceptable for example and a child is condoned for it. What does that teach us as adults? To not express our frustrations and anger in a safe place.

How do we learn to accept our shadow?

Once we are aware that we have a shadow side then we can learn to work with it. I hadn't come across this term until 2018. You can't begin to heal something if you don't know what it is right?

There are a couple of terms which come up when we start looking at our shadow. The first is trigger. When a person does or says something, which evokes a strong feeling or reaction in you, that person is said to have triggered you. Rather than responding to this straightaway, if we recognise it and are aware of it, we can then start to explore it. For example, I am always early for appointments or meetings. When people are late, I feel frustrated with them as I feel they are stealing my time. If I look further into it and delve into my shadow it is also because I am impatient. Impatience can be deemed a negative characteristic. Why can't you just wait for something? But I want it now screams my shadow self. Another term used frequently is projecting. When we become frustrated with another person, or angry, sometimes what we see in them is what we see in ourselves, but maybe don't want to admit. I was reminded of a great question to ask yourself in situations like this. Is this mine or yours?

I had a real pain in my shoulder so went to visit an osteopath. She believed it was related to my liver. The pain in my shoulder was referred pain from my liver. I googled it, as I do with everything! Interestingly the liver can hold repressed anger. I started writing 'what am I angry about? What have I repressed that I hadn't dealt with? What do I need to let go of?' Anger erupts if an individual violates your boundaries or if someone or something stands in your way, thus hindering one's progress or expansion. I had been putting myself into a position where it was easy for me to feel like a victim, which was then making me angry. On the flip side of anger, I see passion. If we think of what our shadow aspects are, then we can look at the opposite end of the spectrum and see what the light aspect is too. For only working with and embracing our shadow can we begin to shine light on it.

ACCEPTING YOUR SHADOW SELF

If you can learn to accept your shadow self you develop self-acceptance, which leads to becoming less judgemental, more accepting of others and humbler. Owning the shadow side leads to a greater sense of wholeness and balance. You become more mature, peaceful and comfortable with yourself. It can increase your creativity. When we can accept and face our shadow, we are then more able to accept and understand others.

Please be aware though that your shadow side is and always will be a part of you. It is what makes you who you are. We can't eradicate it or erase it. Only when we shine a light on the darkness can we embrace the light. And as you work on yourself and heal yourself sometimes the shadow side will raise its head again to allow you to release any more judgements, opinions, limiting beliefs that you may have about yourself or others. However, it does become easier to look at this side of ourselves and recognise it for what it is. Where does the anger come from for example? It may stem from being a child, which is where inner child work comes in, which I will go into later. For now, here are some basic tips to help you work with your shadow side.

PRACTICAL TIPS FOR WORKING WITH YOUR SHADOW SIDE

- Seek counselling or visit a psychotherapist, there are people trained specifically in helping you with your shadow self

- Meditation

- Writing and self-reflection- asking yourself what am I angry about? Why am I greedy? Why do I feel impatient? Why am I jealous?

- Painting or drawing. When you sit down ask yourself what does my shadow side need to express?

If you are working with your shadow do feel free to share your experience using the hashtag #Awakenyoursoul

— 4 —
HIGHER
BEINGS

THE UNIVERSE IS a big place. Maybe that's an understatement. The Universe is a huge place, and for us to think that we are the only living creatures in existence within this vastness would be slightly narrow minded. When I was 18 years old, I was studying for my A Levels. One of these was an AS Level called General Studies. I remember sitting in class and we were discussing how the world began. Some people thought it was the Big Bang theory, others voted for Darwinism. "Does anyone else have any theories?" my teacher asked. I put my hand up. "I believe that we were put on Earth as part of an experiment by aliens" I told him. There was silence for a few seconds before the class erupted into laughter. I didn't outwardly speak about aliens or read much more about them until 2018 when I was guided to a book called Bringers of the Dawn by Barbara Marciniak. As I was reading it there were so many aha moments in it. Things I had said were written in this book. Beliefs I had held that were buried within me and a remembering that there is more to this Universe than meets the eye. There are a variety of higher beings in the galaxy and beyond. The names for these extra-terrestrial beings all come from the constellations. There are Arcturians, from Arcturus. This is the brightest star in the constellation of Bootes. The Pleiadeans from the Pleiades. This is also known as the Seven Sisters and located in the constellation of Taurus. The Sirians are from Sirius, a star of the constellation Canis Major that is the brightest star in the heavens also known as Dog Star. I am sure that there are many other higher beings out there and as they make themselves known to me; I will share. For now, these will suffice. My own experience has been predominantly with the Pleiadeans so I will share my knowledge and experience of those with you first and an overview of the Sirians and Arcturians. In order to understand about these higher beings, I firstly want to share with you what a starseed is.

WHAT IS A STARSEED?

The word starseed recently came into my existence. When I tried searching more traditional dictionaries, I couldn't find the word. I was watching a lot of YouTube videos talking about starseeds and having no idea what it meant. The word starseed is used to describe a soul who has incarnated on planet Earth yet "comes from somewhere else." Tad vague so I carried on looking

Urban Dictionary describes a starseed as, "a person who is spiritually aware, having a strong connection to the divine creator." We talk about our spirit and our soul being within us. When we accept that actually our soul/spirit comes from a galaxy thousands of light years away (sounds like the beginning of Star Wars doesn't it?) we can bring the term starseed into our own existence. Now stick with me. We don't all come from the same star system. If we did, we would all be healers for example, which although would be awesome, we also need people who are more interested in building things for example, or inventing new ways of living and being. We all have our own particular talents which stem from our starseed origination. We can discover our own starseed origination through meditation and soul exploration. This information is also held within our Akashic Records. A book holding all of the information about your soul. You can access these yourselves or ask someone else to access it for you.

SO WHERE DO STARSEEDS COME FROM?

Good question. Starseeds originate from star systems like the Pleiades, Sirius, Andromeda, and Lyra. These are the ones that I am currently aware of, although I know there are more. Apparently, my soul group originates from Nihal but I do have a Pleiadean guide and recently found out I was a Lemurian priestess in my first incarnation on Earth.

WHAT IS THE PURPOSE OF STARSEEDS?

Starseeds generally come to earth with a mission. Starseeds are old souls sent back to earth to assist Gaia in the ascension from 3D to 5D consciousness. From the many starseeds I have seen, their role has been predominantly to plant seeds of spiritual awareness, to support others on and through their spiritual journey and to shine a light for others.

HOW DO I KNOW IF I AM A STARSEED?

When we are born into human form, we generally remember who we were in the first few years of our lives until we can talk. As we cross the four/five-year-old age we begin to forget our lives before and concentrate on learning the experience on Earth. However, deep within us we remember. Star seeds often struggle to fit into 'normalised' institutions, you may tend to rebel against rules and don't always like to conform, you may have a yearning to go home which you can't explain.

10 SIGNS ARE A STARSEED

- As a child you felt that you didn't always fit in

- You're highly sensitive, which you may have been criticised for in this lifetime

- You pick up on other people's emotions easily and often know something is wrong without them having to say anything

- You may have had dreams or memories of past lives and experiences in different dimensions. You may have encountered UFO's or higher beings in your dreams or in meditation

- You know you have a purpose here but may not be sure yet what it is

- People might find you a bit out there, different, weird, strange

- In crowded places you may feel overwhelmed due to so many other people's energy around you

- You have natural psychic gifts, channelling or healing abilities

- You love looking at the stars and the Moon

- You have an inner knowing that you are here to serve the world love and be of service to others, this is your calling

NOW I KNOW I AM A STARSEED OR NOT, WHAT'S NEXT?

If this doesn't resonate with you, that's OK, we are all spiritual beings having a human experience. We all signed up for different reasons to be here. This may not be your path. Yours may be to invent something which moves humanity forward. If this does resonate with you then I would highly recommend meditating to connect with your higher self. It is only through practise and continuing our spiritual journey that we uncover and learn more about ourselves, our spirit and our souls' journey. My recommendations are to stay mindful and present, enjoy what you currently have, work and ask your spiritual army to support you along the way, this may be in the form of angels, spirit guides, ascended masters and your higher self. Ground and protect your energy daily. Raise your vibe and follow what inspires you. Whatever you feel called to will be the tool to assist you along your path.

As I said earlier my main communication has been with the Pleiadeans and I will explain a bit more about them next.

THE PLEIDIANS

Have you ever heard of these beings? I hadn't, until a client of mine saw one. I was giving her Access Bars and she told me she had seen an elfin like face with a crown on its head. I said "maybe it is an elf and you're meant to connect with elementals?" I was so wrong! If you have read my first book you will know that I trust very much in the Universe to guide me along my path. Later that day, one of my students, Lizi, shared a podcast in my Facebook group, Consciousness Arising. It was by a chap called Steve Nobel, who does some fabulous meditations and he was interviewing a lady called Barbara Goldsmith. Barbara was in a trance like state and channelling the Pleiadians. I have heard mediums channel before so I was OK listening to this woman talking in a slightly strange voice. What I mean is, as a channeller, she puts herself out of the way to allow the Pleiadians to use her voice to talk. It may sound out there but it's true. Nearly everything she said,

I was like, I knew that! Not in a big headed, ego sort of way, but in a knowing way. She mentioned that Brexit was meant to happen and Donald Trump had been put into power for a reason. Now I know Trump isn't the most liked character in the world. (Another understatement). However, whatever you think of him, he has shaken things up. We needed to get out of our comfort zone and it's the same with Brexit. It's shaken people up. This was what the Pleidians confirmed through Barbara.

My friend, Jon, contacted me telling me to watch a new programme on Gaia about extra dimensional beings. Gaia is a TV channel that you can subscribe to and there are a lot of spiritual documentaries on there, TV interviews etc. I fast forwarded the episodes to a chap called Rob Gaultier. He was channelling higher beings. He was sat with his eyes closed, talking in a different voice. About 20 minutes in he mentioned something called the Nihal. Something clicked and resonated. I had heard of that before. Racking my brains, I tried to remember. Ten years ago, I had my Akashic Record reading done. Everyone has an Akashic Record. It is a book all about your soul's journey from incarnation to your passing. I mentioned in A Gentle Hug for the Soul about spirit guides from this reading. What I didn't mention as I didn't understand what it meant was that I was told my spirit group is Nihal. I had written it down as Neehar. I ran upstairs and found my journal. There it was on the paper. Neehar. I tried googling it but couldn't find anything. I contacted Rob via Twitter and asked him what it was called. He told me the right spelling. There is a blog where someone channelled the following information:

"Nihal used to be the home star of the Xabinar (gryphons). They are residents of this galaxy who originate on the far side of the Nihal gate. The Nihal gate is an aggregator gateway for species from across the Milky Way, as well as home to a major traffic gateway from the Lesser Magellanic Cloud as well as Andromeda. It is a seriously important hub for spiritual traffic in this galaxy."

Make of that what you will. Having an open mind is paramount in understanding where we have come from and what else may be out there. I would like to bring your attention to the fact that there are other multidimensional beings out there. Having a knowing they are there may bring you comfort in time.

WHO ARE THE PLEIDIANS?

I googled them and interestingly they do look a bit like 'aliens'. They are spiritually very developed. They watch us, observe and communicate with some of us through telepathy. They want to help us, as human beings, to evolve to a higher dimension. They want to help us create a New Earth. Our focus currently on the environment is a prime example of how we are creating a New Earth for future generations to enjoy and live in. The Pleidians are here to help us on our spiritual journey to enlightenment. They are of a 5th dimensional frequency. Earlier in the book I mentioned how we are adapting and moving from the 3D to the 5D, the Pleidians are assisting us with this transition. They are more evolved than us emotionally and spiritually but still working on themselves too. Having this awareness of the Pleidians, is useful in your spiritual journey, so if you encounter them you won't be so scared. They generally come through in meditations or dreams, so don't expect one to be walking down the high street with you quite yet, although who knows in the future.

Their main mission is to help us remember who we are, what are our unique abilities and what our life purpose is. As we raise our vibration through meditation, cleansing ourselves of lower energies and ascending the ability to communicate with these beings can become clearer and you will have a knowing that you are communicating with them. You may inadvertently be channelling their energies also through your words and actions. Through meditation and raising your vibration you may be able to connect with these beings. Sometimes they may visit in a dream. You may be reading this and something resonates within. You may be from the Pleiades yourself.

I have been lucky to have had my own experiences and currently working with a Pleiadean guide called Alkiel, who is bringing information through for me as we go through the quarantine during the beginning of 2020.

HOW DO I KNOW IF I AM OF PLEIADEAN ORIGIN?

There are numerous quizzes online that you can do to find out which star system you originate from. This can also be found in your Akashic Book of records. If you are of Pleiadean origin you may find that you are or show any of the following, this is purely based on my own experience

- You are an empath
- You believe in ET's, aliens, higher beings
- You 'know' reading this that there is some truth in it
- You find yourself saying things and wondering where it came from
- You love being outside and connecting with nature
- You see the connectedness in everything
- You sometimes feel like a square peg trying to force itself into a round hole

- You don't 'conform' to society's expectations

- You rebel against systems, in a peaceful way of course

- You have no concept of time. (I am early for everything and often joke I will be early for my own funeral! I no longer wear a watch; my kitchen clock shows the wrong time as does my car clock)

- You are creative and love writing, painting, drawing, composing, anything that creates beauty in the world

- Your eyes are highly sensitive to light. (Even on darker days I still wear my sunglasses, and in winter lol)

If you feel this resonates you may well be of Pleiadean origin. If not, no worries there are billions of other places your soul/ spirit originated from. Like I said earlier I currently have awareness of Arcturians and Sirians although I have not as yet had my own experience with them. The purpose of those who are of Pleiadean origin is to help others ascend in consciousness and to learn how to live in the 5th Dimension on planet Earth. Sometimes it can take a while to remember who you are and when you do, it can be quite awesome as you begin to learn about another layer of yourself.

Arcturians

My feeling with the Arcturians is that they are a more practical type of being. If you are Arcturian you may be concerned with the environment and sustainability. Here are some traits of being Arcturian:

- You are probably scientifically minded

- You are always looking at ways to improve on existing technology

- You have an inventive mind, creating new ways of working and living for others

- You may have an unexplained love of symbols and sacred geometry

- You tend to communicate using these methods rather than verbalising your ideas and plans

Practical Tips on connecting to your starseed origin.

- Please do not get too hung up over whether you are Pleiadean, Arcturian or from wherever. Learning more about your soul/spirit is part of the journey. When the time is right for you to explore this aspect of yourselves it will come. If you feel ready you may want to try the tips below

- Try channelled writing and meditating which may help you to access them.

- Set an intention before you go to sleep that you would like to have an experience with them.

My biggest piece of advice would be to be patient. Sometimes doing this work takes dedication and patience.

UFO's

There are loads of books out there on UFO's and if it is something you are interested in then do delve in. I wanted to include a snapshot about UFO's as they have been portrayed in the media as something to be scared of. We hear stories of alien abductions, which can bring fear into our minds. The first reported UFO abduction was in November 27, 1896, It was reported in an edition of the Stockton, California Daily Mail, Colonel H. G. Shaw claimed he and a friend were harassed by three tall, slender humanoids whose bodies were covered with a fine, downy hair who tried to kidnap the pair. One of my clients, Maggie, told me her own story. She was travelling back home on the train with a friend and another chap was sat at their table. As the train chugged along something caught her eye. Out of the window was what she described as a small flying object which travelled alongside the window until just before their destination then whizzed off. Her friend saw it and the chap too. None of them could explain what it was. There are a variety of beings in outer space. Some of them are good and some not so good. Just like on Earth. Although I have never been abducted, I have been taken into a spaceship with the Pleidians. When I got inside it was very vast and they had a lot of gadgets. As I looked at them, I saw they had no mouths. In my mind I asked how do you talk then? Telepathy, they told me. Again, I wanted to bring into your awareness that UFO's are real and if you want to share your story with me, I would love to hear it. I interviewed Mary Rodwell, for my YouTube programme, The Spiritual Journey. Mary Rodwell is one of Australia's leading researchers into UFO's and contact phenomenon. Some of the stories that she had heard over the years and the research she has done is amazing. I highly recommend checking out the interview and looking her up online here http://www.youtube.com/Lindsaybanks

WHAT IS AN AKASHIC AWAKENING?

Whereas a spiritual awakening is around remembering who you are and what you are here to do, an akashic awakening is about remembering your own past lives. The word "akashic" is an ancient Sanskrit word that means "cosmic sky," "space," or "ether." When we have an akashic awakening we are remembering where our soul has been and the lifetimes it has lived through. My own akashic awakening came through via writing. I was chatting with my guide, Alkiel and he began to tell me the following

"You remembered you are also from Pleiades and you also remembered your lifetime as a Lemurian Goddess, highly revered for your mystical powers.

What was my name?

Ralesha

Ah I like that name

There were 24 of you within a community. Between you, you governed, wrong word, you looked after so many people. Children, sick and elderly were looked after by the women. The men tended to the crops, built and did what the men knew they were to do. All were aligned with their purposes in life. Time was peaceful. Life was peaceful and much time was spent learning about the natural Earth in terms of crystals, herbs and the natural cycles. This learning is what is being remembered in people now. Gardening and planting seeds, we cheer for that. There will be swapping/energy exchanges and bartering for services. It will start with plants then to other stuffs. Foods, books etc

So, going back to Lemuria, what happened? It sounds idyllic

One man who was sent from upstairs, from a galaxy you haven't yet heard of. He was a being not from our galaxy. He was sent to destroy the peace that was currently on Earth. Intervention was tried by the Council but we were too late. He created a mini retaliation against the goddesses. He whispered words into the men's ears, creating jealousy and anger. Feelings which generally hadn't been felt before. The men not knowing what to do with these feelings reacted with rage and violence. It created a new disparity between men and women. Women were no longer revered by men but despised and looked down upon. It set the stage for the next thousand years and more. This constant battle between genders, inequality, not being good enough and lack of respect between the genders. This awakening is bringing about a change in how gender will be viewed. Mutual respect for the divine feminine and the divine masculine. Recognising within each other the qualities that lie within and respecting them."

I didn't know much about Lemuria so started reading up on it and doing some research. The main difficulty I found was that a lot of the writings on Lemuria are either based on what scientists believe and what channellers have been given. Let's do the scientific bit first. Wikipedia states that Lemuria "is a hypothetical lost land located in either the Indian or the Pacific Ocean" In 1864 Philip Sclater, a zoologist, was the first to develop the theory of Lemuria in order to explain the zoological similarities between Madagascar and India. He believed that long ago there had been a now-lost landmass stretching across the southern Indian Ocean in a triangular shape, which would have allowed lemurs to travel to India from Madagascar. Sclater believed that the land touched India's southern point, southern Africa, and western Australia and eventually sunk to the ocean floor. Shortly afterwards, German biologist Ernst Haeckel claimed that Lemuria was what allowed humans to first migrate out of Asia and into Africa. We then get the first take on it from a medium perspective. Helena Blavatsky wrote a book in 1888 called The Secret Doctrine. In this book she describes information that she received from her ascended masters, her channellings and other contemporary writers/thinkers of the time. These were mostly associated with the Theosophical Society at the time. Helena described these beings as being 7ft tall, hermaphrodite, mentally under developed and spiritually pure. This may have been how she saw them, but it wasn't my experience. William Scott Elliot was a theosophist, who elaborated on Helena Blavatsky's ideas of the Lemurian race. He wrote a book called The Lost Lemuria in 1904. Interestingly, William Scott, was also given information by another medium at the time called Charles Leadbeater. Part of Williams work was scientific and part based on Charles' mediumship. Scott-Elliot located Lemuria in the Pacific ocean. Having sunk it arose to create smaller land masses, what is now the Hawaiian Islands. In his book he delves more into depth about Lemuria and what he was told. There are links to all of the books that I mention at the end. When I found out my story the book, I turned to was The Women of Lemuria by Amber Wolfe and Monika Muranyi. I wanted to know, as a woman, what was Lemuria like. When I read it, most of it resonated and I knew I had been there and been part of it. Essentially, Lemuria was an experiment. What would happen if the Pleidians mixed with the human race? The males were of human origin and the females were of Pleiadean origin. They had babies which were brought up mostly by the females. The women did the teaching and utilised their intuitive skills to help the men know where and how to fish. They knew if there was a storm coming and would advise the men not to go. The men would listen and respect the inner knowing that the women had. I am sure there is more to explore and as and when I am given more knowledge, I will share it with you.

Now we have looked at our relationship with higher beings let's bring things back down to Earth and dive into the relationships we have with others.

6.1.19

When we become one.

When we become united.

When barriers are broken down.

When systems collapse.

When screens are no longer viewed.

When life becomes joyous.

When we become free.

When the 9–5 disappears.

When we make our own choices.

When we become responsible for who we are and what we do.

When we learn to love ourselves.

When we learn to love others.

Truly.

With compassion, gratitude and respect.

When we become compassionate.

Not only compassionate but empathetic.

When we treat others equally.

When there is no longer a divide between rich and poor.

When status disappears.

When the ego has gone.

When we land.

When we appear.

When you truly grasp life.

When you allow your soul to soar.

When you break free.

When we understand.

When we love.

When the shackles have gone.
When we love.
When we learn to fly.
When we learn.
When we love.
Only then.

— 5 —
TWIN FLAMES, SOUL MATES & KARMIC RELATIONSHIPS

26.08.2019

When you look into a person's eyes. Truly look. What can you see?

Can you see their fears, their worries, their past hurts?

Can you see their sadness?

Can you see them for who they are?

Can you see their joy, their passion, their love?

Can you connect on a deeper level than what you see on the surface?

When we allow ourselves to connect on a deeper level, we are also opening ourselves up.

Allowing another to see our vulnerabilities.

Allowing ourselves to be vulnerable to another and allow them to see us.

Truly see us.

How can you connect with someone?

I wrote this following my experience at a festival I attended in the summer of 2019. I had a deep, intense connection with someone there. When I came away, I did what most of us do and slipped into a fantasy world imagining what life would be like with that person, how could we overcome distance and barriers to be together, would we get married, have children, move house. I am sure most of us do this, please tell me it isn't just me! The intensity of the feelings I had were super high. Like nothing I have ever experienced before. It was a physical and energetic connection. I asked my guides to help me explain it and the above words are what I was given. Later that week I was told he was my twin flame.

If you have read my first book you will be aware that I am not really a fan of labels but there is a lot of stuff out there on twin flames, soul mates and karmic relationships so I wanted to include some information for you around these different 'types' of relationships we have with others, specifically love relationships. I have been married once and divorced. I have been in long term relationships and not so long ones. There seems to be a thinking that we meet someone, we fall in love, we get married and stay with that person forever. This may have been the case in the 1800's when people would get married at 18 and die at 28 for example, but with us living longer, is it really fathomable that we stay with one person forever? Often, we have a variety of relationships along the way in which to learn and grow from. Marriage was first introduced in Mesopotamia in 2350 B.C, a ceremony uniting a man and woman. Marriage had little to do with love or religion. Marriage was about the woman becoming the property of the man. I remember reading that the reason marriage was introduced in the UK was because at the time the government or whoever was in power at the time didn't want to pay for women to live alone so they had to get married. I read The Other Side & Back by Sylvia Browne who questioned the future of marriage as we know it. When I got divorced people often asked me if I would get married again and I said yes. However, I wouldn't do it in the conventional or traditional way. I see future weddings more like becoming ceremonies of love. You can state your intent to love that person and they love you. Know that you will be together for as long as you are meant to be.

WHAT ARE THE DIFFERENT TYPES OF RELATIONSHIPS YOU CAN HAVE?

KARMIC RELATIONSHIPS

Some relationships are karmic. This means that we agree to meet another soul at a particular time and space for a reason. You have what is known as a soul contract between you. Sometimes people flit in and out of your life, whilst others stay a bit longer. The main reason that they are in your life is because they are usually the biggest lessons in love. I met my ex-partner on a dating website. As soon as I met him, I knew I had known him before. I knew the relationship wasn't going to be long term. I knew we were going to be together for a reason unknown to either of us at that time. We stayed together for 14 months before detaching and going our separate ways. I learnt a big lesson about boundaries and for me what I will/won't accept in a relationship. It is worth thinking about the relationships you have had in your life to see what lessons they have brought you. Karmic relationships can be your biggest teachers in this life and bring opportunities for your soul to grow. My ex-husband was also a karmic relationship. He taught me, unknowingly, to stand up for myself, to learn to speak my truth, to stand in my power. He showed me how resilient I am, that I couldn't be broken. To be honest, it is easier when you are out of the relationship to reflect and see what lessons that individual has brought you.

How do I know if I am in a Karmic relationship?

- If you notice a similar pattern coming up in your relationships then it is a sign that this is something you have to let go of and break free from

- Often there is co-dependency in the relationship- where you are constantly trying to please the other person

- The energy may feel heavy after the initial honeymoon phase

- If you are questioning the relationship or making excuses for your partners behaviour this may indicate an unbalanced relationship

- If you are in a space where you are being emotionally or physically abused please know that this is not okay. There are some people out there claiming that you are meant to be with them and continue to emotionally manipulate their partners. Seek out a therapist or some support. There are links to various support groups at the end of the book

Karmic relationships don't need to be boyfriends/girlfriends, it could be friends and family too. These karmic relationships can sometimes be linked to our past lives. I touch on this in my first book. In a past life we may have been with our family members before but the roles reversed. For example, your mum in this life, may have been your daughter in a previous life and you have agreed to swap roles in this lifetime to learn a different lesson. Another type of relationship you can have is with a soul mate.

WHAT IS A SOUL MATE?

The word soul mate was coined way back in 1822. The definition is *"a person who is perfectly suited to another in temperament"* Soul mates are people that you feel comfortable with. You enjoy their company, you like spending time with them, they make you laugh. A soul mate is a beautiful connection to have in this lifetime. Again, you have agreed between you to meet in this lifetime to learn lessons from each other. An old friend of mine came back into my life. We had connected years ago at university and had got on really well. When he showed up again it was like no time had passed at all. We got on really well. I went out one day to meditate in a field and asked Upstairs/Source what I needed to know about him. I was told he is your soul mate. A soul mate connection is comfortable, but you didn't come here to be comfortable Lindsay. Thanks guys! We of course have free will in who we date and connect with. Upstairs/ the Universe will guide people into our life for a reason and sometimes it is unknown at the time why. Many couples have chosen to be with their soul mates in this lifetime and are working harmoniously together to both grow personally and spiritually.

With all of our relationships, be it friends, partners, lovers, we have all agreed before we came here that we would meet in our lifetime at certain points in order to learn certain lessons from each other. Some of us may go through abusive relationships. I don't condone abuse of any sort. I was in an emotionally abusive relationship where the words were so cutting and critical that I stopped trying to do things. I stopped speaking my truth as I was shut down for my beliefs and opinions. I couldn't say the 'right' thing or do things in the 'right' way. When I left it, I didn't know who I was any more. I felt lost. Broken. I had to find me again. It took time but I came through it. I healed my heart. I found me. I started speaking my truth again and it felt awesome. I didn't recognise the abuse at the time as I thought it was just the other persons character, their way. It wasn't until I left that a friend said you do realise that you have been emotionally abused? I was shocked. How could I have let that happen? I learnt some big lessons though from it. I have profound inner strength and resilience. I am courageous. I dug deep into my heart and started healing and transforming myself back to me and it felt awesome. It took time and I don't regret the time I was with him at all. He helped me to recognise my own inner light that was shining bright. Now to the final label for relationships, twin flames.

WHAT IS A TWIN FLAME?

The words "twin flame" have only recently started to become more popular. As we are ascending into the 5th dimension there are new words and language coming in. I had never heard of this word until I had my own experience and met my twin flame. When I knew what the connection was, I then began seeking tools to help me work with this. Some of which I will include at the end of this chapter. A twin flame is not the same thing as your soul mate. It is a highly intense spiritual connection.

"Some people say there is no such thing as a twin flame, that we are our own twin flames. In one sense you are a whole flame. When you unite your divine feminine and masculine within you, you become whole yourself. Your flame burns brighter than before"

A twin flame will help you to unite the divine feminine and divine masculine within you. I talk about this later in the book. Essentially a twin flame is your mirror. They reflect back to you all the goodness within you as well as your fears and insecurities. Again, like with everyone else in your life you agree to meet at a certain point and time. This is most likely to happen when you least expect it. I was quite happy in my own world doing my thing. I decided to turn up at a festival one day and boom. We were in a tent dancing. I hadn't really noticed him until we were asked to connect with someone, look in their eyes and tell them something we had noticed about them and how they made us feel. I told him I had noticed his beautiful beard and it made me feel protected. He said he had noticed my eyes and felt protective towards me. Prior to this meeting I had asked upstairs how can you be intimate with someone without being sexual. The next exercise we were given was to either ask for kisses on the neck, a back massage or just to talk. I had been dancing for over an hour in 25 degrees heat so even though I really wanted to ask for kisses on the neck it didn't feel right so I asked for a back massage, as did he. He said to me afterwards, "Just to let you know Lindsay, I think a back massage is more intimate than kissing" My question was answered and I asked if he fancied a cup of tea and a chat afterwards and he said yes. We didn't stop talking and the connection was intense. I didn't want to leave but I hadn't planned to stay and was working on the Saturday. However, I went back to the festival on the Sunday and we met up again. We chatted, played and enjoyed each other's company. Unfortunately, the next day he was heading home, just a few hundred miles away. I felt like I was on an energetic high that day and the following day until I came crashing right down to Earth. Sobbing and unable to get off the settee to get dressed. What was going on with me? Why was I feeling low? I had had this awesome experience and now here I was obsessing about him and not being able to focus on my work or anything else that was going on. Towards the end of the week I discovered, thanks to a meditation, that he was my twin flame. I then googled the life out of it. To understand it, to find tools to help support me through this journey, to find others out there like me. Thankfully I had a friend Paul, who I remembered mentioning a few years ago that he had met his twin flame, to speak to and share my journey and seek advice. He told me how there had been a first wave of twin flame connections back in 2012 and the second wave was in 2020. Interestingly when I googled the definition of twin flame there had been a huge spike in July 2020 of other people looking to see what it meant.

Following the initial meeting with my twin flame I had an intense emotional week. The biggest support I found? It came from myself. My children were on holiday with their dad and he lost his phone so I couldn't speak to them. My parents were on holiday too. I stopped drinking the day after I came back from the festival and wine had been my external crutch for a while. Who could I lean on but myself? I went for a walk to my thinking tree. A tree near where I live with a ladder propped up against it and a chair halfway up the tree. (I think there needs to be more of these dotted around) I find it so still and peaceful. As the wind blew through the trees, I thought about how no matter what external 'stuff' is going on around us, we are our own inner strength and support. We cannot support others if we cannot support ourselves.

If you have to question whether the person you are with is a twin flame then they probably aren't. For what the two of you will experience is unlike anything that you will have experienced before. This isn't about falling in love, for we may fall in love with many over our lifetimes. We may have several soulmates through our life, but there is only one twin flame for everyone, and your twin flame may not even have chosen to incarnate at this time. If they aren't in the physical in this lifetime know that you can still connect with them but on the astral plane. The twin flame relationship doesn't have to be romantic. You can still come together and work together for the greater good.

They are a part of you and you of them. There is instant attraction. Chemistry unlike anything you have ever felt before. It's a physical and energetic and soul connection. You meet and don't want to leave or let go of this person because the connection is so great. In the beginning you may only meet for a brief time. This may be a weekend, a week or a few months even. This brief period allows you to connect and to have that wonderment of what is this? You may feel following this connection like you are on an emotional rollercoaster. You have both agreed to meet in this lifetime to help you both to ascend. To clear karmic cycles. To heal yourselves at the deepest level possible. To both fulfil your mission and purpose in this lifetime. When you thought you had healed everything you could more 'stuff' will come up.

THE SEPARATION STAGE

The feelings between the two twin flames are so intense that a separation period is essential to enable this healing process to occur for both people. During this time know that you both can be there to support each other but there also comes allowance and acceptance. Allow each other space to heal what they need to and accept that whilst they are there, you also need to continue on your own development and healing. During this time one twin flame may be known as the 'chaser' wearing heart on sleeve, wanting to tell their twin flame everything and maybe coming across as full on. The 'runner' may feel intimidated by the level of intensity in the relationship and run. There is quite a lot of stuff on the internet about this and you will know, if you meet your twin flame in this life time which one you are. The roles may even reverse as the chaser in the beginning realises that it is also actually intense for them and they become the runner whilst the other party becomes the chaser.

The separation stage can be extremely challenging. You can't stop thinking about that other person. It borders on obsession! Let go of the outcome and focus on yourself. It may sound selfish to some, but it is an essential part of this process. You may feel you want to speak to them or see them all of the time since your encounter. They may feel scared by the intensity of the feelings you may have for them or the intensity of their own feelings. As may you. This isn't something that you can force. It can feel as if they are rejecting you, but they are not. If they say they aren't available right now, allow them to feel that. If you feel rejected what is that bringing up for you? Can you see how there is work to do during this time?

"Your twin flame triggers all the buried wounds and pain in you"

The best thing that you can do during this time is to be kind to yourself. Eat well, drink lots of water, exercise, meditate, journal, cry, laugh, have some healing work done such as Reiki or shamanic healing. Whatever you feel drawn to. Also be aware during this phase that exes may resurface if there is any unfinished business between the two of you. You may meet someone else or they might. What you have together is very special which can't be felt with anyone else. Your twin flame reflects back to you yourself. Shadow and light. One of you may be extremely emotional, heart on sleeve, I love you, straightaway, whereas the other may hold their emotions back slightly, scared of being hurt. The intensity of the feelings may be too strong so they back off. There is a theory of runners and chasers. Where one twin flame runs away and the other chases. If we think of it more as a dance it enables us to recognise that sometimes one of you will step forward and the other steps back and vice versa. It is a dance of true love. Embrace this experience. It can hurt and it can be an extremely challenging time for both of you, however the rewards will be great.

When I asked 'upstairs' what I needed to know about twin flames this is what I was given

> *"The pain you feel when you're apart initially is unlike anything you may have felt before. Many are meeting and parting at this time. Emotionally you are ready for this. You have reached a point where your vibration is high enough to understand. To not be placing 3D pressures and expectations on them. To allow them to be them. To allow you to be you. To co-exist in a dimension that is new. To co create in a way that serves you both. Yet at the very base of this, at the root is love. Pure love for each other. It is a journey for you both. We aren't saying it is easy as it will ask you to uncover and reveal depths and parts of you unknown to another. Be vulnerable. Be honest. Be open. Love will thrive."*

HOW DO I KNOW IF I HAVE MET MY TWIN FLAME?

When you initially meet there is an intense physical and energetic connection, unlike anything you have felt before. You will know that you have known this person before. You may be given guidance afterwards in your dreams about your connection. You and your twin flame have a telepathic connection. You may be able to feel emotions that are coming up for them and vice versa. Sometimes this may occur in the physical too. I had been planning a weekend away in London for nearly a year, a reunion to meet up with some friends I had been in Hong Kong with. On the Thursday before I was meant to go, I fell over. It is years since I had fallen over and I hurt myself quite badly. I thought that I had broken my ankle. I went to the Dr's after school pick up who recommended I head to A&E. I dropped the kids off at my neighbour's house and drove there. When I entered, they said there was a 5 hour wait. I had no one to put the kids to bed so I said I would come back on the Monday. I came home and asked for healing to be sent to my ankle. I woke up the next day and was able to walk on my ankle and head to London. When I met up with my Twin Flame, he told me how on the Friday he had been at a trampoline park and had twisted his ankle. Same side as me. This might have been a coincidence, but I don't believe in those.

WHAT SORT OF STUFF COMES UP DURING THE TWIN FLAME ROLLERCOASTER?

All sorts of stuff! Deep rooted fears and insecurities stemming back to childhood will arise to be processed and worked through. You will be facing your shadow and learning to embrace it. Connecting to your inner child. Working on matriarchal wounds, patriarchal wounds, ancestral healing, past lives. You can see why the separation stage for some can last for years.

WILL WE COME TOGETHER IN PHYSICAL UNION?

This completely depends on whether you are meant to be in physical union in this lifetime. I know that sounds cryptic. I am aware of some twin flames who have come together and

I am also aware that right now there are some who aren't, myself included. When twin flames come together, they do so to aid humanity in some way, be it mentoring others or building an eco-village for example. Can you see why there is much work to do before coming into union? You need to be able to work on yourselves and healing prior to this so that you are both embracing a new way of having conscious relationships.

You may be reading this and have already met your twin flame and be on that journey. You may be happily with someone and wondering if they are your twin flame or not. It doesn't really matter. If you are with someone, married, in a relationship and you are happy enjoy it. Trying to search out and seek for a twin flame doesn't work. Your journey is your journey and the people you meet are right for you. You are where you need to be right now. If you are in a relationship and you are questioning it or you are feeling unhappy then you have a choice. You work at it or detach from it. There is no shame in detaching. I went through this feeling when I was getting divorced. I felt embarrassed that I couldn't make my marriage work anymore. My ex was a soul mate and taught me that I have an inner strength and resilience that I didn't know I had.

Relationships moving forward are going to adapt and change as we shift our consciousness. We aren't going to be striving for the 2.4 kids, married with a beautiful house. Our perception of relationships will alter as we begin to recognise that self-love is paramount. The old adage "You can't love someone else if you don't love yourself" is very true. How can you have a feeling for someone else if you can't experience that feeling for you?

Total dejunk of the heart

I was doing a reading for the collective when I came up with this term. Can you remember the Bonnie Tyler song, Total Eclipse of the Heart? Well I sang these words to this tune in my reading. What does it mean though? Our heart chakra is where we hold our love. We feel love, give love and receive love. Through not only this lifetime but others, stuff has happened which has meant that we may have created a barrier around it, to stop us getting hurt. Dejunking the heart is about letting go of those past hurts, those relationships which you may be clinging to. Learning to love ourselves is, I feel, one of life's greatest lessons for all of us. It is always easier to show others love through our words and actions than it is ourselves.

How do you dejunk the heart?

Having an awareness that your heart area is your central place of love is a start. You can have energy healing done to remove any blockages within this area.

The biggest lesson we will have for relationships moving forward is that of the relationship with ourselves. The words "self-love" is quite abundant in spiritual communities and sometimes it comes across as being seemingly really easy. Standing in front of the mirror saying, "I love me" is one of the hardest things I have ever had to do on my self-love healing journey. By the 5th time I was in tears. I was saying the words but didn't believe it. Practising self-love is a daily and moment by moment practise. Allowing yourself to choose you first before anyone else can take time to practise. For some reading this you may already be in a fabulous and successful partnership based on trust, honesty and open communication. As we all continue to ascend into higher levels of consciousness our relationships also change. Not only with our other half, but our friends and family. Acceptance is key in this.

— 6 —
CHANNELLERS & CHANNELLED WRITING

UNBEKNOWN TO ME at the time of writing A Gentle Hug for the Soul, I was channelling. Whilst I was attending the Spiritualist church, I channelled William Shakespeare. It shocked me to be honest. Why on earth was he coming through? He gave me a simple poem and then told me that all of the pictures make him look so serious, but he did have a sense of humour! I posted in a Facebook group about it and someone told me I needed to apologise to God. I kindly refused. I wanted to learn more about channelling so spent some time on Google and YouTube to see what I could find. I came across Bracha Goldsmith channelling the Pleidians on YouTube, which was fascinating to watch. I then came across Abraham Hicks aka Esther Hicks. I went to see her in Denver. She was amazing and you can tell that she was channelling another being. Lee Harris channels the Zee's. Rob Gaultier channels Treb. These guys are doing amazing stuff for humanity. Being a facilitator/ conduit for these higher/ extra dimensional beings is amazing!

Barbara Marciniak wrote a book in the 1970s called the Bringers of the Dawn, which was channelled by the Pleidians. One of the first lines started with this and straight away I knew I needed to read more.

"The system is corrupt. It does not work. It does not honour life. It does not honour Earth. If something doesn't honour life or Earth, you can bet it is going to fall and fall big time."

Considering I read this in 2018 and it is currently 2020, we are starting to see this finally come into play. How did Barbara know this though? As a channeller, she had done the work on herself to raise her vibration. When your vibration reaches a certain frequency, it becomes easier to channel these beings. Some people channel through words and some go into a trance like state, a deep meditative state where they allow their bodies and voices to be taken over by higher beings. When you are channelling through writing or speaking without going into trance it is also known as conscious channelling. You are awake and consciously connecting with higher beings to bring through words of love and light for the collective.

Esther Hicks is a lady who 'channels' Abraham. Having seen her in Denver, Colorado in 2019 she is fascinating to watch. Some channellers close their eyes and speak in a different voice. Esther takes several deep breaths then begins. She picks members of the audience to come up and ask her a question. When she replies she has her eyes open and she talks. The words coming out of her mouth aren't the words that she would use. She isn't coming from a place of ego or opinion or judgement. How do I know this? Because when I channel 'stuff' from Source or upstairs they give me words I don't always know or use. Their vocabulary is so much more expanded than ours. When she answers questions, she is coming from a place of love and laughter.

"We are that which you are. You are the leading edge
of that which we are. We are that which is at the
heart of all religions."
—Abraham Hicks

You can find so many inspirational YouTube videos by Abraham Hicks about life, relationships, law of attraction as well as books and they also offer cruises where you can go and learn all about them. Esther and her husband Jerry started speaking with Abraham in the 1980s. They started running workshops with small groups of people and it has grown and grown. In Denver there must have easily been at least 1000 people there. Did you know that The Secret was actually inspired by Esther and Jerry Hicks? If you haven't read the Secret yet it is a must read for anyone interested in the Law of Attraction and manifesting.

When I came away from the workshop, I felt motivated and inspired. The biggest lesson to come out of it was to daydream more. Spend 99% of your time daydreaming and 1% doing. When you allow yourself to daydream you are creating magical thoughts. When you dream big you feel great and when you feel great your vibration rises which allows the manifestations to come in with more ease.

Last year when I was writing my first book, 'A Gentle Hug For The Soul' I did some channelled writing. It was the first time I had done this and I wasn't sure how or what to do. Some people suggest pretending to write or writing swirly lines before you start and words start to become visible and go with the flow. I didn't intend to do automatic or channelled writing. I was stuck on a section of my book. I took myself outside into the garden. I took 3 deep breaths and asked for some help with my book. When I felt ready, I opened my eyes and started writing. The words that I wrote were very general and weren't necessarily words I would write. Does that make sense? This message confirmed my belief that I was channelling messages from other beings:

1.8.2019

We are excited that you have decided to work with us and become a channeller or conduit. The lessons that we are aiming to teach through you are all Universal. This meaning they can be applied to all. Regardless of religion, sex or gender. These messages are aimed at the souls, the spirits of the human beings on this planet. As they rise, they will start to listen. You describe it as planting seeds and yes this is true what you have been doing. A seed planter. The ideas or basic principles to life aren't actually that difficult as they are the principles, they used to adhere to eons ago. They are merely principles to be remembered in this case. The guidance that is currently being sought will be provided through yourself and other channellers around the world. Record your channelled messages and upload them. Send them out into the ether. They need to be shared. To spread light. To shine light. To guide and support others on their spiritual journey. Others will find and support you too as you continue to grow and evolve. Imagine this time last year thinking you would be talking to us. Ooh you would have laughed and denied it. Your work that you have done on yourself continues to raise your vibration and because of that we can speak to you. We shall leave you for now as we can sense your tiredness but we will be back. Byeeee.

As you might imagine this shocked me a bit! How on earth can I be channelling higher beings such as the Pleidians? It was like they said. I had done so much work on myself that I had raised my vibration to a point where it had become easier for their frequency to merge with mine. If we go back to the basics in that we are all energy. As we raise the frequency of our energy we are then beginning to open up to other high frequency energies within and around the galaxy.

CAN ANYONE CONNECT TO THESE BEINGS?

If it is part of your journey to connect with them yourself then yes you will be able to connect. It is within all human beings that they can connect with spirit/their higher self/Source/The Universe as I call it. As your vibe starts to rise then your frequency rises and the Pleidians will be the first port of call as a higher being race that will come into your existence.

HOW CAN WE CONNECT?

Empty your mind. Yes, I know it is easier said than done. Grab a pen and paper. Sit down in a comfy space. Take several deep breaths and close your eyes. Keep focusing on your breath. When you feel you are ready open your eyes and start writing whatever words come into your mind. Even if they don't make sense, don't stop just keep writing. When you feel you have finished, stop. This is the simplest way to channel these beings. They love us and want to share their beautiful messages. Even if you get one word that pops into your head be it love or whatever. Know that the Pleidians messages are generally always full of love and light and are Universal messages for the planet. If you have written something which feels quite personal to you and you wouldn't want to share this may be a message from your higher self or a spirit guide. In my opinion it doesn't really matter who is coming through to you to channel as long as they are of love and light.

HOW CAN I ENSURE THIS?

Do my grounding and protection exercise first. This is essential to connect yourself to the ground of the earth and to protect your energies.

Ground and protect your energy exercise

Channelling can come through in a variety of forms- writing, drawing, singing, creating music. It is often when we do write sing something or play a piece of music and wonder to ourselves where did that come from? David Ditchfield has done some wonderful channelled paintings following a near death experience he had. Before his near-death experience, he was a brickie. After his near-death experience he created a beautiful symphony which you can listen to here https:// soundcloud.com/davidditchfield. This music gives me goose bumps every time I listen to it. He also channelled some beautiful paintings. One of which was a painting of Jesus Christ around Easter time, which I felt was very apt as there was a lot about Christ returning at the time and Christ Consciousness. When I saw the painting, it made me cry as it felt that it had been created through someone else.

My Pleiadean guide, Alkiel, made himself known to me through a drawing. Now I am not the best at drawing so it very much looked like a kid's drawing. When I sat, I asked who am I speaking to and was given the letters to write which spelt out Alkiel. Apparently, he is going to help me write another book. I asked him if I could finish this one first which he agreed to, thankfully!

LIGHT LANGUAGE

As my spiritual journey progresses, I have begun to channel something called light language. There are so many new terms and words coming into my existence that sometimes I struggle to keep up. I have included at the back of this book some terms and words which you may come across in your spiritual journey. Light language is something that came into my existence a few months ago. Last October I was staying with a friend in London and was just about to drift off to sleep when I heard a noise which woke me up. The noise had come from my own throat. It had made like an H noise. To be honest it freaked me out a little bit. I thought no more of it until earlier this year. I was deep in meditation and the noise came through my throat again. How is this possible?? I visited my beautiful friend, Daniela Pala, for a Reiki session in February just before lock down. I was so deeply relaxed towards the end. I heard a word and a voice which jolted me awake. When I asked Daniela if she had heard it, she confirmed that she had. Something was trying to speak through me, or words were trying to escape yet I didn't know what it meant. I had met Susi Jones at a pop-up meditation I ran in 2019. Somehow in 2020 we got chatting about the subject of light language. I had a 121 with her and it activated something within me. A remembrance, acceptance that I was meant to do this. There is no actual definition of this word in a dictionary but how I would define it is this

"Words, symbols, songs and art which are channelled by a person connecting to their higher selves and Source. They put themselves out of the way to allow this information to come through them. When spoken or sung it doesn't sound like anything you may have heard before. When drawn as symbols or art it doesn't look like something you may have seen before. However, upon hearing or seeing this light language your soul remembers it. Your mind may not make sense if it but your heart will."

Light language can be expressed in various forms. Some may appear to be talking in tongues, this reminds me of Harry Potter and parcel tongue! Others may communicate via telepathy or through ESP.

What does light language do?

When you hear someone speaking/singing/chanting light language it can bring many benefits. These include but aren't limited to

- Healing subconscious blockages that you maybe aren't even aware exist within

- Can act as a catalyst for your souls' growth

- Can help you to connect to your higher self

- Can enhance your intuition

- Rapid transformation

- Expanding your awareness

- Remembering your souls' purpose for being here on this planet at this time

These are just a few of the benefits that hearing or seeing light language can bring for your soul and your higher self.

How does it work?

Great question! Light language works on the soul level. It might not make any sense to you when you hear it but your heart and soul will recognise it. You will take what is needed from the session. I started chanting with clients when they were having a 121 session with me and felt drawn to share some in my FB group. It seems to make sense to me and seems to have quite profound impacts on my clients too. One lady on hearing my words said she could feel her heart chakra vibrating.

CAN ANYONE SPEAK LIGHT LANGUAGE?

I believe so. Just like we are all born with psychic and intuitive gifts that when we open up, we can truly access our inner unique gifts that we have to offer the world. By raising our vibration high enough we are tuning into the frequencies of the higher realms. There is also that aspect of letting go of the ego. If you are worried about being judged then you might not share this beautiful gift with the world. I never in my life thought that I would do this, or be using it in my healing sessions. I trusted the guidance I was given and followed my heart. I am meant to do this and share it with others to activate their healing.

OK so where do we go next? You might have read this far and thought that's great but it doesn't apply to me. This next chapter is relevant to everyone. Within each one of us is the Divine Feminine and the Divine Masculine. Read on to find out more.

— 7 —
THE DIVINE FEMININE & THE DIVINE MASCULINE

"Every man has a feminine side,
and every woman a masculine side."
— Paulo Coelho- Like the Flowing River

Within all of us are our own unique gifts, talents and capabilities. There is also within every one of us the Divine Feminine and the Divine Masculine. Embracing both sides can lead to greater health, happiness, presence and a deeper understanding of our actions and reactions to events and people in life. The left-hand side of your body represents the female energy channels and the right-hand side represents the male energy channel, regardless of what sex you identify yourself as. In many different spiritual traditions, the male and female energies are talked about. Yin and Yang, two halves becoming whole. The idea of the God, Shiva, represents the masculine and Shakti, the Goddess, representing the feminine.

What is the Divine Feminine?

There are some words and phrases that have only come into my existence since going through my awakening. This phrase is one of them. I think I read about it in Rise Sister Rise by Rebecca Campbell initially. This was not long after my marriage had broken down. She talked about this feminine energy within all of us. When I was in my 20s being a ladette was trendy. The likes of Sara Cox and Zoe Ball showed us how women could live in a predominantly man's world. Women could go out and drink pints of lager and get drunk just as well as men. Women were trying to fit in. Fast forward nearly 20 years and times are changing. Women are embracing their feminine side again. We are being drawn to gather in circles. The popularity of Red Tents has increased in the last few years. Women are coming together to be women. We don't feel the need to compete. The Divine Feminine is within us all. Male and female. Two polarities. Like right and wrong. The masculine side can be very driven, logical whereas the feminine side can be more creative, nurturing and listen to her intuition. Women have been quashed at times. Made to adapt and fit into a mould that a patriarchal society has tried to fit them into.

Eckhart Tolle mentions in his book that the ego is much stronger in the male mind than the feminine. For women it is easier to let go of the logical and society that has been created for us. When I talk about the Divine Feminine it's not about having long beautiful flowing hair and wearing long robes. It is about discovering that side of us that wants to create, to love, to nurture.

Whilst reading about the Divine Feminine I came across this sentence which really resonated with me so I wanted to share it.

"By connecting humanity to our common inheritance and cultivating self-love as the gateway to universal love, the divine feminine offers a radical recalibration of values and relationships that can reshape our world."
—Temple of the Way of Light

I just want to clarify that I am not saying that women are taking over the world and there is no role for men anymore. Men are also being asked to look within and embrace their feminine side just as much as women and vice versa. It is about balancing both energies within ourselves. When the energies are out of alignment, we can feel stuck, lost, not entirely sure of who we are. Working as an intuitive healer has helped me explore my feminine side so much more. When I went into my first graduate job with a major retailer, it was a dog eat dog world. It was competitive and tough, and male dominated. I wore a mask to work. I couldn't be seen to be weak. I just went in and got on with my job, striving to be the best I could be, working long hours and actually ignoring myself. Ignoring the person, I truly was inside. I was working there because having graduated with a degree in International Business this was what I felt I was meant to do. I got burn out. I was stressed and finally went for some healing. This was the beginning of my healing process.

I was first made aware of the different energies within me when I had my Soul Plan done, with Jude Robinson. She told me that I would be successful in business as I could bring in the logic and decision making of the masculine but balance it with the healing and compassionate side of my divine feminine. As my intuition has grown stronger over the years, I have learned to listen to what my body wants and what my soul craves. Walks in the fresh air, sitting under the light of the Moon, singing out loud in the car and dancing like no-one is watching (even though they sometimes are) As I have been working with the Moon, the natural rhythm and cycles are in flow.

Embracing our feminine side doesn't mean we have to wear swishy skirts and have long soft flowing hair. It is about learning to trust our intuition and our inner knowing, that was built into us from the moment we were born. Since time began women have been persecuted for their beliefs, their witchery, their clothing choices, their birth choices. When you feel persecuted you shut down, you lose your voice, you don't want to stand up for yourself or others.

Let's embrace and support each other, as well as ourselves. The friends you have currently around you. Embrace them and lift them up. Give them a compliment. If you like someone's outfit tell them, or their hair, or their shoes. Doing this raises your vibe and theirs too. And we could definitely do with some higher vibes in the world. Be there for them. Listen to them. Don't try to fix their problems by giving them solutions. Allow them to be them. This is important for both men and women. In years gone by we have masked the feminine side of ourselves by trying to be more man like. Competing with each other. Drinking pints to keep up with the men and show them that we weren't the weaker party. Women in a men's world, playing a man's game. Thankfully, I feel as if we are coming full circle and many more of us are beginning to embrace our feminine side, men and women.

When I was growing up there weren't many strong female role models to emulate, that embraced their feminine and masculine side. Margaret Thatcher was in power at the time and she was definitely more in her masculine power than feminine. It is only in the last few years that I have found some fabulous examples of fearless females. Women living in adverse times who followed their intuition and their calling. Women who embrace their divine feminine, the intuitive and creative side, but also their divine masculine, the doing and taking action to create change. One of these ladies was Molly Brown. You may remember her from the Titanic movie. She was the loudest lady on the ship. Whilst in Denver I visited the Molly Brown house Museum. Born to Irish Catholics in Missouri, she decided to move to Colorado at 18 to live with her siblings. She married James Joseph Brown and had 2 children. Her husband struck gold and they became millionaires overnight. Margaret Brown spent a lot of time giving back to the community. She ran for Senate several times but didn't get in as women didn't have the vote at that time. She was instrumental in helping women achieve the vote. Colorado was the first state where women got the vote. She taught herself several languages and was fluent in them. In 1909 James & Margaret signed a separation agreement. This was at a time when divorce was frowned upon. In 1912 Margaret Brown was travelling in Egypt when she received a telegram to say her grandson was ill and she needed to get back home. She boarded HMS Titanic. When it began to sink, she was annoyed at how few people were in the boats and started telling the crew they needed to fill them. Apparently, two men then picked her up and dropped her 4ft over the edge into a lifeboat. She was with 22 women and 2 men. She told them that in order to survive the night they would all take it in turns to row the boat to keep warm. When RMS Carpathia came to rescue them, all of the passengers in her boat were alive. Once on board she helped translate for the 3rd class passengers and organised a fundraiser for the survivors of the ship. She wrote down the names of the families who were donating money and a list of the families who weren't. She then left this list in the dining room hall.

Eventually those who weren't donating decided they wanted to and their names were crossed off the list. Margaret Brown raised $10,000 from this. When she arrived back in New York she raised another $10,000 and was made president of the Titanic Survivors Association. She decided quite late in life that she wanted to be an actress and went off to train in drama. She became the actress that she had always wanted to be. In 1932 she passed away in her sleep. Having visited the house and reading what little I did about her, she came across as a strong and independent woman in her time. A woman who wasn't afraid to rock the apple cart. A woman who spoke her truth, in a time when most didn't like to hear the truth. A woman who refused to wear a corset and instead took up boxing in her garage! A woman who I believe inspired many and continues to do so to this day. I left the museum feeling inspired. If Molly Brown could do what she did in the early 1900's what can we do now?

We can speak our truth.
We can rock the apple cart.
We can inspire.

How do I access my Divine Feminine?

- Tap into your emotions and allow yourself to feel every emotion, whether it be joy, sadness, fear, anger, love

- Love your body and everything about it- this can take time and practise but talking kindly about yourself and your body allows you to listen to your body more, what it wants and needs

- Learn to listen to your intuition and trust yourself

- Speak your truth- I am a huge advocate of this as it is so liberating! Saying no when you don't want to do something, not being a people pleaser but being a you pleaser

- Listen to music and dance
- Read books on the divine feminine and start to reclaim your power

What is The Divine Masculine?

However, you identify yourself as in the 3D world, we all have within us the Divine Feminine and The Divine Masculine energy. The Divine Masculine side of us is the practical, logical side. It is about getting stuff done and taking action. It represents leadership and strength. Courage. It is about not coming from a place of ego but truth and honesty. Leading without greed or ulterior motives. As a woman I feel my divine masculine energy is around setting boundaries for myself and others. In order to look after myself I need to be strong and have respect to be able to say no. The common misconception is that divine masculine is inherent to the male population. Whilst trying to research this topic there is very little that has been written about it by itself. There are Divine Masculine traits which include logic, reason, action, strength, adventurous. When you research the Divine Feminine, there is a lot more books and articles that have been written. We all have the Divine Feminine within us and the Divine Masculine, Yin & Yang. Some days I feel very much in my feminine energy, feeling creative and inspired, writing, dancing and nurturing myself. Other days I feel very driven to take inspired action, to be doing, to be sharing with the world my creations, to be standing up for not only myself but others, to be leading. To be in one energy all the time feels unbalanced. We can't always be in our feminine energy or things won't get done and likewise we can't always be in our masculine energy as we may miss intuitive signs telling us where to go next and how to move forward. When I attended a festival in 2019, I loved the meditations and the dancing and the chatting but one thing which really drew me in was something called the Spartan Warrior training. I felt this was something I needed to do. Now I'm not exactly very physical. I like my Yoga, and trampolining and gentle exercise. This was completely out of my comfort zone but def felt that I was embracing my masculine energy. We were doing squats, running in the heat, making warrior style sounds, crawling on our bellies under human tunnels and finally wrestling. Yep, myself and another lady, Sarah, wrestled each other. Never done that before and unless the opportunity presents itself again and I am feeling in that energy I probably wouldn't do it again. But you know what? I loved it! I fully embraced my masculine energy for the session. It was tough and felt hardcore. Martial arts are a great form for embracing our masculine energies within as they are often structured, make you feel physically and mentally strong.

For men and women learning to bring both their divine feminine energy and their divine masculine energy into balance brings union. When we achieve union of the masculine and feminine energies, we can achieve our fullest potential.

PRACTICAL TIPS

* Meditate to connect with your divine feminine and divine masculine side of yourself

* Listen to yourself

* Do something competitive

* Go out into nature

* Take responsibility for your own actions and your own life

- Look at your relationship to both your mother and father- how has this impacted you as a person

- Trust your feelings- what do you feel inspired to be or do

- Do something physical

Recognising that within all of us we have both these energies can help us learn how to honour them and trust that when we are feeling in one particular energy, we embrace it. Both energies are necessary for us to feel balanced and at one with ourselves.

— 8 —
SHAMANISM

"We have to discover the shaman within"
—Alberto Villoldo

SHAMANISM IS AN ancient healing tradition and for many shamanic healing practitioners a way of life. Not only is it about facilitating healing work but also about connecting with the Earth, with nature, with animals and every living and breathing thing around us. Using sacred rituals and instruments in their work they are often, in my experience, very humble and kind. Shamanism or the word shaman comes from the Tungus Tribe in Siberia, in Russia and it was coined by anthropologist who went there.

My friend, Katharine Lucy Haworth, had been training in shamanic healing with a lady in London called Imelda Urquhart and was offering guinea pig sessions. It was the first time I had really heard of shamanic healers and thought I would see what was involved. She welcomed me into her home with a cup of herbal tea. It started off with lots of smudging, aka burning sage sticks. Katharine gave me a basket which had been made by girls and women. So beautiful. I had to place it over my stomach and say what I wanted to let go of. I wanted to heal the matriarchal line in our family. It was very emotional and I began to cry. Katharine asked me if I could see a colour and I said yellow. She then went into the garden and picked a dandelion for me. I had to hold it whilst she invited spirit guides and everyone in. I was asked to focus on where that particular feeling was, to pull it out and push it into the dandelion. Katharine then wrapped it in a tea towel and went outside. She said she felt as if she had been tapped on the head by a bamboo tree. Around this tree were panda pictures and figures. I told Katharine that I'd bought a large wall sticker for Eve before she was born of a mummy panda and a baby panda. Katharine told me the panda was one of my power animals, which I go into a bit later on. I called in my spirit guide, the Native American Indian and I felt as if Lisa was sat next to me with her arm around me. I felt as though the pain was in my solar plexus. I felt as though because of this it had weakened my throat chakra and that the two were linked. I'm hoping to have let go of blame I feel. Katharine also did a lot of drumming around me and rattle shaking. Following the session, I felt a lot calmer and like something had shifted in my relationships. I made some dandelion tea, which can help to cleanse the liver. Katharine also sent me a tarot card later that week which she had pulled for me. The Emperor, Arthur. My grandads name was Arthur. The next day was the Grand National. It has been a tradition in our house every year since I was a kid to put a bet on a horse. Well there was one running called One for Arthur. I put £20 on him to win as I saw it as a sign. I have never betted that much before. I won £340 as Arthur stomped into first place. I also received a beautiful Herkimer diamond from Katharine, which can help you connect with the ethereal realms. Having a shamanic healing session with Katharine was extremely healing for me. At the time I was going through my divorce and it was an emotional time. I will always be grateful to Katharine for the session and the path it has led me down.

In 2018 I saw something on Facebook which caught my eye. It was an advert to go and birth your own shamanic drum. How cool is that? I chose buffalo skin. It is all sourced ethically from India. No animals were harmed in the making of the drum. It was extremely tough to actually build and after I had chosen my skin my teacher told me it is the toughest skin to work with but I loved it. I had taken my own crystal to put in it but chose instead a beautiful fire jasper crystal. This signifies putting fire into your belly and passion. A shamanic drum is one of the most important tools for a shamanic healer. You can buy shamanic drums online but I knew I wanted to make my own. Putting time, energy and love into an instrument that could then be used in my healing work. Setting intentions as I was making it to help me to be of service to others. Plus making your own instrument is kind of cool right?

"The space or gap between the drum beats, the sacred geometry, becomes the vehicle for the spoken prayer to ride on out the to the creator"
—*Native American Proverb*

When I first brought it home, I didn't really know what to do with it and didn't want to make too much noise for the neighbours! Over time I became more confident with it, playing it for myself in meditations and others in their healing sessions.

Drumming is an ancient act of meditation. The drumming uses a repetitive rhythm that works up to three to seven beats every second. After around ten minutes of listening to this our human brain waves can change their usual beta state to a more Theta/Alpha brainwave state. We become more open to receiving intuitive messages and opening up to our subconscious. You feel calmer and more relaxed. When I have used the drumming in my 121 work clients have reported feeling the vibrations of the drum within and through their body. Using this in addition to crystal healing and Reiki can be very powerful. I have also found using the drum and speaking light language has had a powerful impact on others physical and energy bodies. Anyone can make their own drum or buy one. Be open to trying it and you never know where it might lead you.

"No-one can heal you; you heal yourself"
—Alberto Villoldo

POWER ANIMALS

WHAT IS A POWER ANIMAL?

I first heard of power animals about six years ago but like with everything else they started to become more prevalent and relevant in my life as my spiritual journey progressed. The first time I connected with a power animal was when I went off to make my shamanic drum. The lady running the course took us on a shamanic journey, where I saw a pink flamingo. To me the flamingo represented balance and fun. Balance as it can stand on one leg and not fall over. Fun because it is pink, vibrant and so different to a number of other birds. I love the fact that I have a flamingo at the moment. I see them everywhere! Be a flamingo amongst a flock of pigeons is one of my favourite phrases that I am seeing everywhere. And I am certainly trying to be!

I ran a Reiki share and as I closed my eyes the first thing I saw was hedgehogs, rolling down a hill. I wanted to burst out laughing as I thought 'how random!' The pink flamingo then made an appearance again. I took this as a sign that I needed to have more fun in my life and more balance, as I have been working quite a lot recently and I do need to have more fun in my life. The hedgehog symbolises someone who is highly intuitive. It can encourage you to listen to your inner wisdom and guidance. You intuitively know the right thing to say. You have a calm attitude to life. When everything else appears to be crashing down around people you maintain a huge sense of inner calm. You are probably gifted with a great stamina, just like your spirit animal.

Everyone has a power animal. Your power animal can change over time as you grow and develop. These animals can be mammals, reptiles or insects. They may also be mythical creatures such as unicorns or dragons. You can connect with them through meditations or shamanic journeying.

My friend has a dog, Louie. Now apparently dogs can also have their own power animal. My friend had been on a shamanic course and the shamanic teacher had told her this. She asked the teacher if he could connect with Louie's power animal. The teacher rang her the next day and said Louie's power animal was a grasshopper. When Lisa came home that afternoon there was a grasshopper on Louie's food bowl. She had never seen one before and hasn't seen one since that day. Coincidence?

Power animals are an important part of shamanic work. Christa MacKinnon describes them as providing the shaman with, *"power, wisdom, guidance, teaching and protection in the physical as well as spiritual worlds".* For me, having an awareness that there is at least one power animal with me, gives us greater insight into our own being and spiritual outlook.

SWEAT LODGES

I truly believe that the Universe conspires to put you in the right place at the right time for what you need. A beautiful friend of mine, Jote Prakash Singh, posted on Facebook saying that some Mexican shamanic healers had arrived at the Sanctuary they run. Did anyone want some shamanic healing for a donation? I posted it into my Facebook group, Consciousness Arising and several people said they were interested. On the Monday I had arranged a physical meet up for said group. It was going to be in a central location in town. One of the guys in my group, Paul, suggested we meet at the Sanctuary instead. Great idea!

On a fairly warm Monday evening we arrived at the Rising Dawn Sanctuary. A fire had been lit in the grounds and we sat with a cup of herbal tea chatting. Several members of the group went for the shamanic healing whilst we chatted about synchronicities and the Universe. Nam Prakash, who ran the Sanctuary, asked me if we would like to stay for the sweat lodge ceremony which was happening later that evening. Five of us said yes, we would love to. After about an hour finally one of us asked what is a sweat lodge and what do we have to do. Basically, you take your clothes off and sit on the ground next to a fire whilst you sweat. It didn't exactly sound appealing but I am always up for new experiences. Luckily there were some towels to protect our modesty as some of us weren't quite prepared to be half naked in a tent full of strangers.

Tai, the Mexican shaman, had built the sweat lodge with natural twigs and thrown blankets over the top. It looked like a short-domed hut. A fire had been lit not far from the sweat lodge. Within a sweat lodge you always have a firekeeper and Tai's daughter Sunflower was it. Tai and his daughter,

Sunflower led us through a beautiful ceremony thanking the four elements, Earth, Wind, Air and Fire. The women were invited into the lodge first.

It was dark outside as we undressed, placed the towels over certain places and headed in. As you enter you say an ancient Toltec phrase to give a blessing. There is a hole dug in the centre where the hot rocks would be later placed. We crawled around the hole, slightly ungracefully. There were lots of ow's and ouches as we stood on twigs and rocks. Thankfully I had brought my cardigan in which provided some cushioning for my bum on the hard ground. There was some giggling as we entered, more from nervousness as we had no idea what to expect.

The men were invited in after the women. We sat in the darkness whilst the rocks were gradually brought in and filled in the hole. A herbal blend had been stewed which would later be poured on the said stones to create the steam. As I sat half naked in this dark tent, I was giggling to myself. The members of my group will never want to come out with me again! Eventually the last rock was placed in the centre. The makeshift door was closed. Pitch black. Tai started chanting and warbling, using his throat to make these beautiful sounds which resonated within and around you.

As the herbs and water were placed onto the hot rocks the steam hit your face. It was quite intense at first and caught the back of my throat, which made me cough. As it subsided and the next lot of steam hit my face, I became more used to it. We were encouraged to deep breathe and you could feel your sinuses clearing. In my mind I could see my Native American guide standing with me on a cliff edge pointing at the land and telling me to claim the unclaimed land. I could feel my body and my face dripping in sweat which made me feel cleaner and more purified. The basic idea behind sweat lodges is that they are to help purify the mind and body. I lost track of how long we were in there but by the time we came out and got dressed it was after 11pm. We gave thanks by the fire and everyone said how they had felt. There was a Full Moon bright in the sky and I truly felt as if I had been part of something special. I told the guys in my group how proud I was of them for saying yes to something that they had no idea what it was and for joining me in my crazy adventures!

A sweat lodge is a Native American tradition where a hut is basically built and it feels like a sauna inside. Eons ago it was traditionally a space for men to go monthly. As women menstruate monthly and cleanse themselves, it was believed that men could cleanse themselves in a sweat lodge. It is intended to be a space where you reconnect with upstairs/source. It has physical benefits as well as mental and spiritual healing. Depending on where you are at mentally and emotionally, I would highly recommend connecting firstly with the person running the sweat lodge to ensure you are in the right space to do it. There are numerous places that you can attend sweat lodges across the world. I would always recommend getting in touch with the people running it first to make sure it feels right for you. I wanted to share an overview of the experiences that I have had myself over the last couple of years. There is so much more that can be said around shamanism and there are some fabulous books on it, which I include at the end of this book. However, I feel that for the purposes of this book it is suffice for me to include a chapter and direct you to other resources if it is something you have a calling for.

Practical tips for connecting with your inner shaman

- Seek out a local shamanic practitioner- they can guide and teach you

- Read more about shamanism- there is a list of useful resources at the end of this chapter

- Do a course on shamanism

- How can you create your own rituals in your daily life?

One thing that shamans do is speak to their ancestors which leads us nicely into the next chapter on ancestral healing and past lives.

— 9 —
ANCESTRAL HEALING
& PAST LIVES

I WROTE IN A Gentle Hug for the Soul about past lives and my own experiences of these. Naively, I didn't think I would have much more to say on this in this book but as my own journey continued so much more came up that I needed to share. It began with buying a pack of oracle cards called Angels and Ancestors. For two weeks in a row I was getting the Elder card. It talked about forgiving my ancestral line and how my ancestors were sorry for any hurt that I was suffering now because of them. I then had several clients where past life 'stuff' was coming through for them. As I was facilitating healing sessions, I began to see in my mind's eye their past lives. Helen had a healing session with me and kindly allowed me to share her story. From the very beginning of the session I felt as if there was a little witch with me. I could then see Helen working as the Witch's apprentice. They were together in a small hut mixing herbs. I could then see Helen being taken away by a group of lads and I was told she had been persecuted as a witch in a past life which was why she was struggling with her throat chakra in this lifetime. I removed a lot of 'stuck' energy from around her throat area. As I relayed the story to her after the session, she just stared at me. "Oh, my God", she said, "I was at a past life workshop a couple of weeks ago and I found out I was a witch's assistant and persecuted by a group of young lads who had me by the throat". That threw me too to be honest. I had had experience of a spirit guide coming through once before but I had never brought someone's past life into a healing session. The theme of this carried on as I brought through the past life of one lady as a Roman warrior goddess, then a chap who had been in the stocks and stolen food for his family so ended up in iron shackles in a prison cell and left to die. His ankles and wrists were in the stocks and he suffered arthritis in his hands and feet in this lifetime. I then wondered if I could access someone's past life in person, could I do it via distance? I asked for several guinea pigs in my group and sure enough I could see their past lives and tell them who they were and how it was affecting them in this lifetime. Our past lives are embodied in our auras. Everything that has gone on before is in your aura. Healing these ancestral lines and past lives can really help to free us in this lifetime. It can help free us from fears and phobias as we come to understand why we have those fears currently. The line of our ancestors is a long one. Never before has there been a time, such as now, that we are healing them as much as we are. Remembering and accessing the past lives of our soul can help us realise who we are as a multi-dimensional being.

> *"Where traumas, problems or strong types of behaviour have occurred with one or other of your forebears, the energy from this experience gets passed on to future generations."*
> —David Furlong

Thankfully what we seem to be seeing in 2020 and moving forward is people healing themselves, their ancestral lines and their own past lives in order to heal future generations. When we begin to see that there is more to us than a mere mortal enjoying one life, that we are a multidimensional being enjoying the facets of life, we begin to realise we have a lot of work to do in terms of healing. Not just for us but for those who have gone before and those who will come after. For our children let's heal the past and allow them a lighter, freer future so they won't carry the burdens from years gone by.

Lindsay

When I want to write I choose

My tools for the job in hand

With a feather in one hand

And a pot of ink by my side

I feel as though I'm taken back

To years gone by

The scratching of the quill reminds me

Of being a girl at home

Lying in bed convinced that there was a ghost writer in my room

Maybe it was the future me

The one I now am

The writer, sitting in 2019 with

Quill and Ink

Was it me? Was it the knowing of who I was to become?

I wrote this following my dad bringing me a feather quill pen he had found in his garage. We can all access our past lives through meditations, hypnosis or finding a reputable therapist. If you do decide to have one done, I would love to hear your story. #Awakenyoursoul

I spoke to Stephen Towill for my YouTube programme, The Spiritual Journey, about lives between lives. Where do we go between our lives on Planet Earth? This is something that he specialises in and has many great stories from clients to share. I experienced something similar a couple of weeks ago. I was doing a past life healing session for a lady. She was in the 1940's then we went back to around 1880. When I asked where she was in between I was told that she was on Planet Earth but not in the physical sense. Our soul/spirit whatever you want to call it has lived many lifetimes on this Earth and this is in your energy body, your aura. Often people ask if this will be their last lifetime on Earth. Your soul decides when it returns to Source whether there will be a next time or now.

HOW CAN YOU HEAL THESE ANCESTRAL LINES, KARMA AND PAST LIVES?

• There are a variety of meditations that you can do on YouTube that can aid you with some of these.

• You can visit hypnotherapists to have past life regressions done. These show you who you were in a past life.

• Book in for a session with myself at www.lindsaybanks.uk

— 10 —
The Universe:
signs & symbols

Feathers often symbolise that Angels are nearby. Pennies can be reminders from loved ones. I've also heard of buttons from our dearly departed. But what other signs and symbols can you look out for? Why are they important? When I was having doubts about my own path and life purpose I kept hearing a song by Swedish House Mafia and the main lyrics I kept hearing were "Don't you worry, don't you worry child, cos Heaven's got a plan for you". I was like OK I'm listening. Part of this spiritual journey is learning to trust that upstairs/the Universe knows so much more than we do.

We are a small piece of this vast cosmos and even though we do like to think we know best and where we are headed, there can be a bigger plan at work. Bigger than we can often imagine. This is where the Universe signs come in.

I was driving back from Glastonbury and the main A road was closed. I got diverted and is often the case all I had to rely on was my sat nav on my phone. As I drove along the solitary, single land roads I was questioning if 'it' knew where we were going. I had nothing else. No road signs. No maps. I had to trust it. The sun was setting and two baby deer's ran across my path. Two hares appeared and ran across my path. As I drove slowly along another hare ran alongside my car with me.

I finally got home about 20 minutes later than expected. I thought nothing more of it until a friend posted on her Facebook page that she had been out walking and seen a hare too. Bear in mind, I have never in my life seen a hare! I looked up the meaning of it. The basic meaning of it was rebirth. If a hare crosses your path it means prosperity and abundance in the future. "Wow that's cool" I thought. A week later I was doing my cards for the week and pulled a card from Kyle Grey's Angels and Ancestors pack with a hare on it.

Another hare! The message was very similar. A time of rebirth and to see all of the seeds that I have planted to be sown. How cool is that? I have also been craving water over the last couple of weeks. Drinking it and bathing in it. So much so that I went for a full immersive swim in the North Sea. Something I have never done before. It felt amazing! It was effing freezing but afterwards I felt tingly and super proud of myself for taking the plunge! Especially since I myself have had a fear of drowning since I was little. In a past life I was an Indian man who did drown. I did it though!

Now I haven't always listened or agreed with the Universe/ Upstairs. I wrote a blog post in June 2019 about getting into an argument with the Universe which I wanted to share with you here.

I decided I had had enough. I wanted off the spiritual train and wanted a 'normal' life. I told it (the Universe) that I didn't want to be a conduit. I didn't want to be a messenger. I didn't want to tell people about all of this 'out there' stuff that I have been learning recently. Who am I that they will listen to me? I don't want to be the weirdo. The odd one out. The person that people might think has gone slightly crazy. I wanted the learning and knowledge to stop. I felt out of my comfort zone, which I am prone to do. I felt overwhelmed by the knowledge I was gaining. I felt like I couldn't handle anything else the Universe was throwing at me. I cried. Seriously. Going beyond Reiki and crystals and stepping into this unknown voyage towards multi-dimensional beings and life on other planets freaked me out. I had a moment on the stairs whilst I was singing my kids to sleep when I thought, I am such a small part of this world that goes way beyond this earth. I can't stop the path that I am on. I can't choose to unlearn everything I am learning. I can't argue with the Universe, well I can and it may hear me BUT I love to share my knowledge with others through writing and speaking. That is my path. I may be able to pause the train sometimes but I have to keep going. I chose this path so on I go.

When I wrote this, I was feeling annoyed and frustrated that I was learning all of this awesome stuff, but not really feeling like I could share it anywhere. I was afraid of what people would think. Would they think I'm crazy? Weird? Since then I have learnt to embrace it and put myself out there regardless of what others may think. This is my journey. My path. My calling.

The Universe sends you signs in different forms. Animals, numbers, symbols, people. Several people may mention the same word or name or comment to you. Take note. The Universe has your back and wants to help you forward in the right direction. To live your life on purpose. When we face resistance and have to battle or fight, it can sometimes be because we are going the wrong way, or we aren't quite ready for it. When we think about where we want to be and where we are headed, our logical mind kicks in and when the 'thing' we wanted doesn't happen we can feel disappointed or frustrated. If we feel we have an idea of where we want to be and possibly an overall vision, but are open to more going with the flow signs and synchronicities will appear. For example, I had booked a flight to Denver, Colorado. Two days later I happened to be watching a YouTube clip of Abraham Hicks. Normally the video comes up with Abraham Hicks, and a subject title. However, this day when I looked at the screen it said Abraham Hicks, Denver, Colorado, May 18th 2018. That's funny I thought, I am heading there May 19th 2019. I wonder if she will be doing another event there. When I looked it up, sure enough, she was going to be in Denver, Colorado at the same time I would be. I booked a ticket. To be at one of her events is truly inspiring and I would highly recommend anyone to go if you have never been. If I hadn't been open to the Universe sending me that sign or being intent on having such a structured plan in place, I may never have had the opportunity to see her work.

Look out for the signs and symbols for you. Often, what we want is for like a huge billboard to appear from the sky with writing on it or for a loud voice to tell us what to do next. This doesn't happen. The signs come through more subtly. The reason is for you to begin to trust the Universe/upstairs/ source. Signs come through in a variety of ways. Through conversations. For example, if 3 different people all happen to mention Reiki in a week, then maybe you should be giving Reiki a try. Or if they all say you need to speak to John Smith, then you need to speak to John Smith. Pay attention to songs which come on the radio.

Some people keep seeing numbers. I talked about angel numbers in A Gentle Hug for the Soul and what they mean and have included them here for you. This is a basic guide and there are a variety of numerical combinations which can all mean different things. If you keep seeing the same numbers, I highly recommend that you write them down and look up what they mean.

Angel Number 1 encourages you to look to new beginnings, opportunities and projects with a positive and optimistic attitude as these are appearing in your life for very good reason. Your angels want you to achieve and succeed with your desired goals and aspirations so do not hesitate in taking positive steps and striving forward. Do not allow fears, doubts or concerns to hold you back from living and serving your Divine life purpose and soul mission.

Angel Number 2 may also be a message to display compassion, diplomacy, consideration and adaptability as you passionately serve others in your day to day life. Your angels are encouraging you to pursue your life purpose and soul mission with faith and trust in the Divine.

Angel Number 3 is an indication that your angels are trying to get your attention. The angels and Ascended Masters want you to follow your intuition and inner-wisdom so that you are able to take appropriate action at this time. Use your creative skills and abilities to manifest your desires and enhance your life and that of others. The angels encourage you to follow your life path and soul mission with optimism and enthusiasm.

Angel Number 4 is an indication that your angels are offering you love, support, encouragement and inner-strength, enabling you to do what you need to do and achieve your goals with diligence and proficiency. When you take positive action towards your highest intentions, aspirations and goals, the Universe works in your favour and helps you to establish solid foundations and advance you along your path.

Angel Number 5 brings a message from the angels that important life changes are upon you and these changes will bring about many positive opportunities for you. The angels ask that you look upon these changes with an optimistic and positive attitude as they are destined to bring you many long-term benefits. Remember to be grateful for the auspicious opportunities ahead of you.

Angel Number 6 brings a message from the angels to keep a balance between your material goals and aspirations, and your spiritual, inner-self. Respect yourself and others by taking responsibility for your own life and be honest and fair in all of your dealings. Be grateful for what you have already, as an attitude of gratitude encourages further positive abundance into your life.

Angel Number 7 tells of a beneficial time with obstacles overcome and successes realized. Your angels are happy with your life choices and are telling you that you are currently on the right path. You are encouraged to keep up the good work you have been doing as you are successfully serving your soul purpose and life mission and your angels are supporting you all the way. Positive things will flow freely towards you, and this will assist you along your journey.

Angel Number 8 brings an uplifting message of encouragement from your angels telling of achievements, success, striving forward, progress and attainment. It is a message to stay optimistic and listen to your intuition and inner-guidance as you hold positive expectations and thoughts of positive abundance in all its forms. Set solid foundations for yourself and your loved ones as this will ensure your future prosperity. The Universe and your angels will always support you, but it is your responsibility to ensure that you put in the appropriate work and effort when and where necessary. You are encouraged to live up to your full potential.

Angel Number 9 is a sign from the angels that your life path and soul mission involve being of service to humanity through the use of your natural skills and talents. It suggests that you are a natural lightworker and encourages you to look to ways to serve others in positively uplifting ways. It may be indicating that it is time to end a phase, situation or relationship that is no longer serving you in a positive way. Rest assured that 'new' will enter your life that will enhance and benefit your life and lifestyle in many ways. Prepare yourself today as there is much work for you to do.

I continue to see repeating numbers at certain times in my life which bring messages. You may see numbers in sequences or constantly waking up at a certain time. Look up what these numbers mean and make a note. Take the message that is coming through.

Animals can sometimes come through to us in dreams, in real life or images. If you keep seeing a particular animal what characteristics does that animal have? For example, a lion. When you think of a lion what comes to mind? Strength? Courage? Bravery? If you aren't feeling particularly strong right now the lion is bringing that strength in for you.

PRACTICAL TIPS

- Ask for a sign from upstairs. Then ask again and again until you have heard them or seen it

- Notice things which stand out to you, e.g. a feather in your kitchen, how did it get there? Someone calling you out of the blue. Hearing the same song

- Write down what these things are and what you feel it means to you

I would love to hear what signs or synchronicities you have seen in your life! Share them with the hashtag #Awakenyoursoul on IG or Twitter

— 11 —
MANIFESTING &
LAW OF ATTRACTION

*"Fearing rejection is rejecting the best possibilities
and opportunities that are presenting themselves to
you now"*

I FIRST CAME across the Law of Attraction when I was
introduced to the movie The Secret by Rhonda Byrne. I then
went and bought the book. This was back in 2009, right at the
beginning of my spiritual journey. I remember at the time
thinking well it might work for them but there is no way it
will work for me. I read a few more of her books and thought
a similar thing. In The Secret, the people talking about their
successes were actors and athletes, not a retail worker like
me at the time.

The Law of Attraction is the belief that positive thoughts
bring back positive things and negative thoughts bring back
negative things. Napoleon Hill was also very familiar with
this concept when he wrote his book, Think Rich, Grow Rich,
way back in 1937. One of the main principle teachings from
studying the successes of millionaires and businessmen in

his book was that thoughts become things. I touched on this in A Gentle Hug for the Soul as I too, started to become aware that I would have a thought, write it down and within a matter of time, sometimes 24 hours, sometimes a few months, these thoughts could become reality. If it was as simple as thinking a thought and it coming into our existence, then we would all be living the life we want. However, in order for the Law of Attraction to work for you, you have to believe in it. If you are sat there thinking, like I did over ten years ago, it isn't going to work for me, guess what you are telling the Universe. It isn't going to work for me. If you are open to giving it a try and believing, it starts to work, then when it works for the first time, you are surprised and like, wow. If your mind is full of thoughts that you can't do this or that, then you won't do this or that. If your mind is thinking I'm not good enough, that is what you are telling not only yourself but the world around you. If you tell yourself I believe in me and I am worth this then it lifts your energy and therefore your vibration.

Affirmations have become extremely popular. The reason being, I believe, is that more people are seeing the benefits that positive affirmations are having on those around them. By repeatedly telling yourself I believe in myself, for example, rewires your brain. FYI I am not a scientist so can't prove this scientifically, however your mindset does change. You go from a place of thinking I can't do that, to a yes, I can do that frame of mind. Surrounding ourselves with newspapers, bad news and negativity can seriously impact our thoughts. Remove these from your life and it will start to improve your mindset. Look at the relationships around you. Are your friends fairly positive, uplifting people or do they criticise you and talk down to you? Hanging around with people who aren't raising your vibe or lifting your energy will bring you down too. Hanging around with people who love and support you for who you are will lift you.

Energy from the heart resonates at a higher frequency than the brain. When we are using the law of attraction to manifest, we don't always receive what we want. Why? Because our heart isn't really in it. To engage our heart before our heads will bring better results, and quicker.

"Thoughts are vibrations. A practised thought is a practised vibration=reality"
—Abraham Hicks

I started practising manifesting again when I started my business. It began with a vision board. On my vision board I had pictures of a woman having fun, the words published author, Soul & Spirit magazine as I wanted to be in the magazine talking about crystals. In December 2017 I appeared in the magazine talking about how crystals helped me get through Xmas. Over time the pictures have changed as things have come to manifest. I had a tent on there in 2017 as I wanted to take the kids camping. It was the smallest picture ever! In that same year we went to a festival and camped for three days. I had a trampoline on there and several days later a lady posted that she was selling her 8ft trampoline, which I bought. I popped affirmations on there to remind me I am always in tune with the Universe. Having that visual to remind us of our dreams and goals allows us to bring it closer into our reality.

In 2019 a trip to America trip came about through manifesting. I wrote down on Facebook that I wanted to go to the U.S and 2 weeks later I was invited. I will explain what happened prior to this so you realise it wasn't magicked out of the air, but a series of steps had been taken to orchestrate this, more or less. Following the launch of my book, A Gentle Hug for the Soul, I then was looking to market it. I LOVE Twitter and one day when I was on there, I came across a lady called Lanette, and her company was called Women with Gifts. She was doing some Twitter lives and asking people to send copies of their books to her and she would review them. Awesome. I contacted her and sent a copy over to her in the U.S. I already had a copy on U.S shores, Oprah hadn't replied when I sent her a book, so I sent it to Lanette. About 2 weeks later she reviewed it on her Twitter live feed and website. She then messaged me asking if we could have a Skype call. It was scheduled for after I had written my Facebook post. At the time we weren't Facebook friends so she wouldn't have seen what I wrote. Anyway, we have a chat and she asked me if I would be interested in writing a chapter and collaborating with her and some other women authors for a book called Women are Roses. I'd love to, I replied. Awesome, can you come over to Colorado Springs in May 2019 for the book signing and an award ceremony. Erm yes, I replied! Wish granted! I booked my flights. The kids were with their dad at EXACTLY the same time I wanted to go over, which worked out beautifully. Not only that but when I booked the flights, I didn't really pay much attention. I'm not one for small details but I knew I had an eight-hour stopover on the way back. For some reason in my mind I thought it was New Jersey. My geography isn't great either so I had no idea where this was in relation to Denver. For 2 years I had had a picture of the Statue of Liberty on my vision board. When I rechecked my flights, I realised my stopover was in NY! I spent 4 hours in this fabulous city exploring and seeing the sights.

Now sometimes when we manifest 'stuff' we don't always know what is going to happen in the meantime. I wanted to share my story about a beautiful lady I met and stayed with in Denver, Colorado. Then I will get back to the manifesting 'stuff'. I booked an Airbnb with Nicole for four days in Denver, Colorado. I didn't want to stay in a hotel by myself where I didn't know anyone and she had a dog called

Winston, an English bulldog. (A year later Winston Churchill turned up for a chat with me, but that's another story) On arrival we headed out to Denver Botanical Gardens with another girl staying there, Bella. During a thunderstorm the three of us were sat under some trees. Nicole started to tell us her story. She was running late on September 11th 2011. The day of the Twin Towers tragedy. As she was on the ferry heading to work, she noticed that there was smoke coming from the tower next to where she worked. She thought that maybe a helicopter had clipped the tower. Apparently, that was quite common! As she got off the ferry and started walking towards work in her $400 pair of shoes, she noticed what looked like a huge dust cloud. She felt an arm grab hers and turn her around to face the other direction. The next five hours were a blur. She somehow made it back onto the ferry, covered in dust and dirt. At the other end she was hosed down. She didn't know what to do, where to go or even what was happening as all communication was down. A kind elderly gentleman approached her and offered her a cup of tea at his apartment. She went with him. He tried calling her mum several times on the phone, gave her numerous cups of tea, fed her and gave her some clean clothes. As she drove to her mum's house, she said the highway was eerily quiet. What should have been a ten-minute journey took her over 3 hours. Flags started to be hung from apartment windows. She had no idea what was going on. The radio stations weren't working, there was no mobile phone reception. She got to her mum's house who finally told her what had happened. She then went to collect her son from day-care. When she got there, there were still children whose parents worked in the towers, who hadn't yet been collected. She picked up her son and took several other children home with her to look after until their parents came back. The next day she realised she wouldn't be going back to work. The second tower she was heading towards had collapsed. She didn't have a job to go back to. She retrained as a teacher and worked for several years in some of the toughest schools. She currently works as a social worker helping homeless ladies and is an online entrepreneur. Hearing her story, I felt sadness but I also felt inspired. She was part of a hugely traumatic event and she decided she wanted to help others. I share Nicole's story because I felt I was meant to be in her home and visiting her at that time. She had recently lost her husband, the love of her life and she said that the people coming to stay with her were all very spiritual people. When you follow and trust upstairs you never know who you will have the pleasure of meeting or the experiences you will have.

I wrote a list in 2018 of 39 things to do before I am 40. In 2017 whilst going through my Dark Night of the Soul, I was sat at home watching the Killers on TV. I danced like crazy around my living room. I had first seen them in a tiny venue in Manchester back in 2004. I posted on Facebook asking how old you had to be to go to Glastonbury and if I was too old. No age limit I was told, so going to Glastonbury Festival was added to my list. About a week after coming back from America I looked through my list and wondered what was next. Three hours later my friend, Felix called me. "Hey, I've got a ticket for Glastonbury, do you want to come?" OMG!!! Every inch of my mind, body and soul was screaming yes. Would my ex look after the kids? I messaged him and thought if he says no then the kids are coming with me. He said yes. The Killers were headlining. I arrived at the festival with no idea of what it would be like. In my 38 years on this planet not once had I ever felt the urge to go to a festival. But this was Glastonbury! I had to go. It was hot when I arrived, and I hadn't realised it would take me a good forty-five minutes to the tent from my car. I was hot, sweaty and had heat exhaustion by the time I arrived at the tent. My friend had already arrived and kindly put it up for us. I was extremely grateful for this. We quickly met and off I headed with a small map in hand. No idea really where I was going. I located the main stage, found some shade and sat down to listen to Janet Jackson. Personally, I wasn't feeling it so headed off on a wander. As a newbie to festivals I loved it! I had no idea who Stormzy was, or Lizzo or even Slim Thai (a rapper who was later nominated for a Mercury Prize Award) Even though I didn't know the songs the messages from these guys were soooo powerful! Stormzy had a way of bringing people together through the content of his music, his passion and his drive. Lizzo was all about self-love and self-beauty. In the crowd we were all telling ourselves I love me, then turning to our neighbours and telling them I love them. Slim Thai organised a mosh pit and at the end told everyone we never leave anyone behind. I also told my friend that I liked how he was channelling his anger in a productive way and that I was pleased our younger people had some inspiring role models. When I said this, it did make me feel old! There were so many people there though, different ages from babes in arms to those in their 70's. They were all connecting through the music at this festival. Not only is it a showcase for musicians and talented artists but it is also a space where you can leave your life behind and escape into a magical world of love, peace and music.

Driving back from Glastonbury on the last day of June 2019 I stopped at my friend Jon's for a cuppa and some dinner before driving the three and a half hours back to York. I was 45 minutes away from home when I noticed they had closed the main road. My sat nav took me on a detour. I was relating this to a friend later that day and this is how I interpreted it. I wanted to go along the main road as it was the quickest way to get home. My feet were aching, I felt dirty and couldn't wait to get home to get into a nice, salt bath. (The road is our head/ego) There was nothing I could do about it. My sat nav (inner intuition) took me on a route that I had never been down before. I trusted my sat nav (inner intuition) to get me home. At one point I stopped and took a photo as I was driving down a single country lane, surrounding by fields, with no signs. Nothing except my sat nav to guide and direct me. I didn't have a choice BUT to trust it. I could have turned back but the road was closed. I had to keep going forward, not knowing what to expect on this detour. Suddenly two baby deer ran out of the field ahead of me and stopped on the road (I wasn't quick enough to get my camera) I stopped the car and they ran off. I carried on driving and saw two hares dash across the road. I saw the sun setting over the fields and again stopped to watch and admire it. Then another hare came out of the bushes and ran along my car as if showing me the way. When your path takes you somewhere that you didn't necessarily want to go down, it doesn't mean it will be the wrong one. There may well be beauty waiting for you along the path that you (your ego) didn't want to take but your inner you knows, that this is the right direction for you. The next day I pulled a card from Gabrielle Bernsteins oracle pack, The Universe has your Back. I thought it was completely apt.

"Obstacles are detours in the right direction"

I began working with the Moon cycles back in January 2018 and this has amplified my manifesting. Once a month I sit down and set my intentions for the coming month. When I first did this, one of my intentions was to go onto the TV or radio and talk about crystals and/or Reiki. Three days later my friend June emailed me asking if I want to go onto YO1 radio to talk about crystals! I ended up with a six-month guest slot, where I did a tarot card reading, chatted about angels, the law of attraction to name but a few topics. I have manifested opportunities that had previously seemed out of reach, appearing in national magazines, podcast interviews etc. Every Full Moon I do a ritual for letting go and forgiveness and that then creates a space for my New Moon intentions to come in. Learning to work with the moon cycles is fairly simple and once you begin you will carry on doing it as you see the effects. I have created my own moon rituals that you can work with as a basis going forward. These are included at the back of the book.

Getting back to the Law of Attraction. If you can imagine that there is a huge storage container with your name on it. Everything within this storage container is your hopes and dreams and what you would like to bring into your reality. You write your list of what you want to bring in. The people working at the storage facility hear and feel your desires. They start bringing it out of storage. Note our manifestations do not always appear straight away. Manifestation works through a combination of belief and inspired action. If you want a Porsche it is not going to drop out of the sky. There are steps you will need to also take to create this opportunity. I remember Dougie Weake asking me this at YO1 radio. For Xmas that year I bought him a matchbox Porsche. It appeared but not in the way he probably visualised. If we can hold onto the belief that our manifestation will come and take steps towards it, it will be delivered.

If I can do this, so can you! Let me know what you manifest #Awakenyoursoul

Practical Tips

- Create a vision board and place somewhere you can see it-choose photos and pics of what you want in your life.

- Tell yourself I am, what you want to become. I am an author, artist, whatever it is for you

- Believe that you are a cocreator of your life with the Universe

- Start working with the moon cycles- you can find out more about how to do this in my online store www. lindsaybanks.uk/shop

A NOTE ON PASSING TO THE OTHER SIDE

I couldn't finish this book without a note on passing to the other side. This last year has opened me up even more to the spirit world and beyond. My mediumship skills have developed and this continues to bring me insight and clarification that there is more to us than this lifetime. Death is not something to be feared. It is a transition to the other side. I have helped spirits who were stuck to move over this year. One Sunday morning I woke up and a friend had tagged me in a post on Facebook. It was a video of a couple driving along, and on their webcam, they had caught the image of a young lad walking along the grass verge. It was after 11pm at night. I kept watching it and felt that there had been a horrific accident. Less than three miles away and three years earlier there had been a hit and run. A driver who had taken copious amounts of drugs had hit two young lads from behind. This was the spirit of one of the young lads. I sat and tuned into his energy. He didn't want to pass over as he was worried about his mum. He took me to the scene of the accident and I sat holding his hand as he relived the memory. We got up and began walking towards a tunnel of bright white light. Two people came walking out of the tunnel towards him. It was his grandparents. They opened their arms and he walked towards them to a full embrace. He turned to look at me, thanked me and walked into the tunnel with them. I sobbed for ten minutes afterwards. Sometimes spirits haven't fully had the chance to say goodbye to loved ones and can be hesitant towards going towards the light. If we know in this lifetime that that is where we are meant to go and we can communicate from the other side then at least when we pass, we can go in peace.

MICKY'S LEGACY

This morning I was visited by an old friend. Nothing unusual with that you may be thinking. Maybe, but this friend passed over around twenty years ago. I was told he had passed from a heroin overdose. I haven't thought about him in years. I used to work with him and we were good friends. All of a sudden, he was in my mind. The image of him wouldn't dissipate so I got up and came downstairs to write. This is what he said,

"I chose to end my life as I was in a dark place. I couldn't see a way out. My childhood wasn't great and as I got older, I chose to numb my emotions with alcohol (He's sat next to me smoking a cigarette as he tells me what to write) It started with alcohol and I thought that was enough. I could block out the memories and the pain. It worked when I was drunk but when I wasn't drunk, all of that was still there. I didn't know any of this stuff that you do Lindsay. It wasn't even on my radar. I started taking/using heroin as it brought me a sense of relief, even more than the alcohol. I felt I had achieved something in my life. I had learnt how to deal with the pain. I know now I hadn't but it felt like that to me. One day I thought I'll take a little bit more, just to see what happens. That was it. I passed. I remember standing over my body, my shell and feeling such a sense of peace, like I'd never felt before. I felt free. I didn't feel sadness or pain. I turned and walked away from myself. I saw my grandad waiting for me. He embraced me and we walked through a tunnel of bright white light.

I went into like a movie theatre to sit down and watch my life in replay. The good bits and not so good. You were in it and I want to thank you. I realise that I wasn't capable of loving anyone else as I couldn't love myself. You always treated me with respect and kindness. Thank you. I am now helping others who are at that edge, who may be suffering and feeling pain. Where I can, I am signposting them and sending signs to where they can find help or talk to someone. We aren't born to suffer or be in pain. I am more equipped on this side to help others on Earth, than I was on the Earth plane. (I asked why he came through) To say thank you and to let you know that there are a team of us spirit side working also on healing the suffering and pain on Earth. Keep up the good work!"

We were friends for a short period of time and whilst I was writing this, I did feel very emotional.

During the coronavirus many people died without the love of their friends and family around them. Whilst I was sat in a mediumship circle Jon came through and he wanted to share this with me, to share with you

When we die, do we die alone? Jack came through to let us know why we needn't fear dying alone. This is what happened. I was on a Zoom call sat in a mediumship circle. I had my headphones in and as we went into relaxation, I became very aware of the thumping of my heart and the boom boom, boom boom noise it was making. In my mind's eye I could see clearly a life support machine and a gentleman lying in a bed. He had an oxygen mask on and was alone. He told me his name was Jack. Suddenly I heard the machine flatline. I asked if anyone in the group could take this gentleman. Nobody could. One lady suggested that it may have just happened. Sometimes this can happen with spirits. Before they transition to the spirit world, they visit someone. Normally it is a member of the family but Jack came through with an important message. He was still with me when we finished the group chat so I asked him if he wouldn't mind helping himself to a cup of tea whilst I did an interview and as soon as I finished, I would chat with him. (You know sometimes when you think life can't get any weirder than it is right now, and you're speaking to a spirit in your house asking him to make himself a cup of tea!) These are Jacks words

JACK, AGED 64

"I needed to speak with you as I have recently left my body. I am aware that there will be many people at this time dying alone. Without their friends, family or loved ones nearby. I wanted you to share this message as I feel it may bring comfort to someone on the earth plane. Although it may be perceived that when we pass, we are alone this is not true. In my case, my wife had passed before me and she was there to embrace me. My parents stood side by side ready to embrace me too. Before I join them on the spirit side I was told to connect and bring this message to you to share. Physically your loved one may be alone when they pass. Spiritually they are not. What I felt when the machine flatlined was like an all-embracing feeling of love. I wasn't scared or panicked. I had this knowing that I was going home. I was safe. Loved. For anyone worrying about their loved ones at this time, I hope this message brings reassurance. Tell those you love that you love them every day. As we are all born, we all die. I will leave those words with you to share. I will now make my transition to the other side and leave you in peace. Thank you for my tea. Goodbye"

He walked out my front door with a wave back. I cried for a short while conscious of the emotions being felt around the world at this time and the wonderful gift Jack had left for others.

If you have read A Gentle Hug for the Soul you will know about my friend Lisa. A very close friend of mine, Lisa, passed away on my 36th birthday in 2016. I've heard very little from her except when she turned up once at the Spiritualist Church and told me off. I was really annoyed that the first thing she did when she came through wasn't to give me any advice but to tell me off! I was at a festival in 2019 and was sat in a playful mindfulness workshop. There was around ten of us sat in this tent with our eyes closed. I was sat listening to Ryan's voice, the chap leading the meditation, when I suddenly felt her next to me. She was a very playful character. I spoke to her in my mind. "What are you doing here? I'm trying to meditate" She just laughed and started pulling funny faces at me. I was really pleased to see her but I was trying to concentrate in stillness and she wasn't helping. "I can do this now" she said. "Do what?" I asked her. "This, I have been practising and I have learnt how to communicate from the other side" I smiled as she danced around me. She brought up some memories we had shared. Dancing together in a pub, drinking wine and laughing. She told me some stuff I needed to hear. I started to feel extremely emotional as I left the tent. Ryan was still talking. I knew I couldn't sit in the space any longer. As I left the tent and started walking away, I started to sob. You know when you start to cry and you find yourself gasping for breath. Gut wrenching, huge sobs. I had been so pleased to see her but I seriously wasn't expecting her to drop into the middle of a field when I was at a festival. Luckily, I bumped into a lovely lady I know, Kitty, who steered me into her tent and helped me work through the sobbing and emotions I had been holding in. I realised in that moment that I had never really grieved for her and I needed to see her to let it all go. Since then she has appeared intermittently sending love and reassurance that I am on the right path.

When our loved one's pass, they leave a space in our physical lives, but they leave a gift too. Of their love, their time and the memories that you have together. Know that you will meet your loved ones again when it is your time to make the transition.

The patriarchal system that has been in place for so long is finally beginning to crack

— CONCLUSION —
A NEW EARTH

12.2.19

We are ready for change. Embrace it.

We are ready to rise. Do it

We are ready for fun. Live

We are ready to honour

We are ready.

It is our calling.

Our place in the world has been found.

We check in.

We embrace.

We honour.

We love.

Let's gather.

Let's connect.

Let's live.

Let's grow.

Let's communicate.

Let's arrive.

Present.

In the moment.

Calm.

Collected.

A collective.

Peace.

Tranquility.

Calmness.

Like a still pond.

Embrace this true.

Embrace the oneness.

Embrace love.

Embrace desire.

Honesty.

Truth.

Enough.

You are enough.

The world needs you to stand, to change, to embrace and honour your gifts.

HAVING LOTS OF 'stuff' came from the deprived years of rationing during WW2. There was scarcity and lack in terms of materials. The 50s and 60s brought new technology and innovation into people's lives. The 70s was all about love and peace. The 80s and 90s were about having it all. The 00s and 10s have been very technology driven. We are living in a completely different world to the 50s. Materialistically we can buy anything with a single click. We can buy, generally, anything we want. Yet there is something missing. Something that you can't buy. And that thing that is missing is connection to ourselves and to others. It is love. Love for yourself and for others. We are heading towards a new Earth, a new way of being and I for one am fully looking forward to seeing what this will look like.

When I asked upstairs about our structures this is what they told me

Why are we investing our time and energy into a political system that we don't agree with? If we don't like the political parties don't vote. Create a new way of leading/being.

The NHS doesn't need financial support. It is mismanaged. Too much money at the top. Overburdened and overstretched. Therapists/Healers will be required to step up and forward next year. People will be required to take personal responsibility for their own health.

I feel it is nearly time to finish this book. It has been a time of exponential growth in terms of my personal, emotional and spiritual development. As I continue to grow, I will continue to share the tools that have helped me so they may also help others. I share my story so that you can see how these tools can be applied in your own day to day life. I have pushed myself so far beyond my comfort zone, it has made me feel uncomfortable. Not only physically, but mentally and emotionally. What keeps bringing me back is my innate trust and belief that everything happens for a reason and the Universe/Upstairs/Source (replace with whichever word you feel apt) knows so much more than me. My mind will want to do something, my heart may want to do something else and I am learning to trust my heart rather than my head.

Everybody deserves to be loved. Everybody deserves to be happy. For that is why you are here. TO enjoy. To have fun. TO laugh. TO laugh brings joy. Joy heightens our senses. We laugh. We rise. We are joyous we rise. Find the small pieces in this world that bring you joy and feel in your heart the love that is possible from that one small thing. Love and honour you and the love and honour from another then becomes possible. Have fun.

My spiritual journey will continue, as will yours. I hope I have provided you with an awareness of tools which may help you through your journey as they have mine.

Namaste

APPENDIX:
CHANNELLED
WRITING

TIME is relative. TIME cannot stop. TIME.
And?
I didn't feel like going out today
AND?
I'm tired
AND?
I don't feel there's space in the house
AND?
I didn't sleep well last night
AND?
I haven't eaten enough fruit
AND?
I haven't drunk enough water
AND?
I wanted an afternoon nap

AND

Fresh Air

AND

My boiler is broken

AND

I need to look after me

AND

Rest

AND

Rejuvenate

AND

Make time

AND

Be kind to me

AND

Love me

AND

Accept the things I can't control

AND

Be happy inside

AND

Be Calm

AND

Be

26/02/2019

Beyond You.
Beyond the Sea.

Beyond the Land.
Beyond the Moon.
Beyond the Stars.
There is More.
More than you can physically see.
More than you can physically hear.
More than you can physically touch.
So much more than the senses you are currently using.
Beyond there is More.

18/03/2019

Wake up, Wake Up and Look Around
The Earth and the Ground
Are suffering because of you
You have treated it unkindly in the past
Now is the time to make a change
Protect your environment, keep it clean
Recycling isn't enough
Start at the point of origin
What are you buying and why?
Do you NEED it?
Can its materials be broken down, back to the soil and the earth?
To the manufacturers of the large organisation
There is an ethical responsibility you have
You can begin to make the change
Buyers can only buy what is provided in shops or by small businesses
You are the instigators, the changers, the makers

It is YOUR responsibility to stop churning out mass manufactured plastic products

The tide is changing

We love that children are getting involved; it is their future planet after all

They don't want to live on a dirty planet

They are inspiring the older ones to change, to listen

Their following will grow until large businesses are forced to listen

$\backsim$

18/03/2019

When one begins to create

They begin to live

Creating is the ultimate joy in life

Creating a picture, a painting, a product

Allowing your mind to settle and focus on the job in hand

What you won't realise is that as you create, you are channelling

You are channelling the energies of us, of those who have been before

We work with you to create beautiful works of art

When the words come seamlessly that is us

When the painting flows that is us

We want to help you create beautiful things on this Earth

Be it a book, a sculpture, a painting

When you have passion and purpose and enjoy what you do, the creation comes easily.

The more difficult bit can be sustaining

Our energies intertwine and mix with yours.

$\backsim$

02/04/2019

My counsel

My counsel

What am I meant to know?

Learn the art of surrendering to life, to love, to the Universe

Be still, Rest and pause, Reflect, Be still

Leave your worries to one side

They aren't worries in this moment

At this minute. This second.

Enjoy. Be happy. Create. Love. Inspire

⁓

15/04/2019

If everyone knew their potential the world would be a much happier place.

One person's needs and wants will never be the same as another's.

One's path will never be the same as anyone else's.

How we feel love is not the same to someone else.

When we become at one with ourselves, we become calm, we be.

Being, the art of stillness, surrendering.

Allowance-to be at one.

The Universe knows where you are going and why you are here.

It sends the signs.

It sends the people.

Opportunities present themselves to you.

It is up to you to say yes.

Don't question it.

Trust yourself and trust in yourself.

Be in the moment.

Appreciate the beauty, the sounds, the love, the people, the relationships.

At one with you.

22/04/2019

The Age of Ascension

What is that?

A time to rise. A time to live. A time to come together. To support each other.

The continuing collapse of "traditional" businesses mean for many they will be forced to find themselves.

To explore their passions and their reasons for being.

Eventually we will go back to how you all started.

You have your own trade or skill that you use to help others.

You may exchange services and have a universal currency.

The currency will be for products and or services.

For example, 2 hours of your time = a 2-hour coin that you can then use for another service.

If you have made a product depending on the time it takes you to make it will depend which product coin you get.

The sunshine will help you all to grow.

Enjoy it.

Embrace it.

Absorb it.

11/05/2019

When the Sun begins to Shine
When the Skies are Blue
Lift your heads to the clouds
And be thankful you're You
For there is no-one else like you
You are unique
You are loved, you are lovely, you are love
When the Sun begins to Shine
When the Skies are Blue
Lift your heads to the clouds
And be thankful for today
Who knows what will come?
Who knows what events will unfold?
All you can do is be true to you
Think of your values
How will you respond?
When a spanner is thrown into your works
How do you carry on?
Take a deep breath and be True to you
We love you. I love you. You love you.

13/05/2019

What is my soul craving for?
Nurturing for me, to nurture myself
Only when I can care and cater for
My needs will someone then come
I feel so content and at peace

In this moment Right Now
Can you Hear that?
Be still and listen
You are hearing the sound of the World
Tune in and connect
Listen to your heart
Listen to your Soul
When you are being true to you
What are you craving?
Not the next iPhone or material good
What are you craving?
Not the latest designer trainers
What are you craving?
Enjoying the richness of Beauty
Stillness? Silence? Peace? Calm?
What are you craving?
Love, honesty & truthfulness
What are you craving?
Connection with others
Connection with Yourself
Connection with Spirit
Stop. Listen. Wait
What you are craving you can find within
What you are craving can't be bought

~

20/05/2019

I want you to take a walk through the desert
What do you see?

Pyramids (Not man made)

A palm tree (Not man made)

Sand (Not man made)

The sky (Not man made)

The sun (Not man made)

Now imagine walking along a beach

That is man made

Instead of sand there is plastic

Instead of an ocean, sewage

Imagine night and day could be switched on and off with a light switch

No more sunrises or sunsets

Those of you who are choosing to save the planet

Are doing so from a place of love

Of love for our planet

We also show love t ourselves and other human beings

We care for the welfare of the next generations

For too long has the earth being neglected

To nurture, respect and love our Earth

Is also to nurture, respect and love ourselves

10/06/2019

I WANT TO BREAK FREE (When thinking about being on Universal Credits and in the system)

Live the way you would as if you're not on universal credit

Don't focus on the money

Focus on living your life how you want to

Experience and enjoy

When you experience and enjoy it, you're vibrating higher

It's easier to attract what you want into your life

Do what you love

Enjoy those moments.

Be mindful

Show gratitude

10/06/2019

Loneliness vs solitude

I often feel a need for solitude. To have time alone with my thoughts.

Time for me.

For my imagination to wander.

Time for me.

To have a bath.

Time for me.

To meditate.

Loneliness is different.

Loneliness comes when we have a want to be with other people.

A want to be sociable.

A want to connect.

It is part of our human nature that we socialise.

Solitude is choosing to spend time alone.

Loneliness is feeling alone.

When you have a faith or belief in the Universe or God or Source you never feel alone.

You just have a knowing that you are protected.

That there are Angels/Spirits/Guides around you keeping you safe.

Solitude is a choice.

Loneliness isn't.

Not everyone is comfortable being alone.

Why? Because they are not comfortable with themselves.

They can't rest or be happy in their own company.

The more time you do start to spend with yourself the happier you will become.

⌒

17/06/2019

Peace.

The peace that is within.

Is there. Seek it out.

It must be remembered that you all have the capability to find and restore peace.

In your hearts.

It is not an external thing to go and find.

It is within you.

To seek the peace within first you must find stillness.

None of this franticness and doingness that you like to create.

Just be.

Allow moments to happen.

Allow situations to occur.

Responding or reacting instantly to these can cause more friction in our lives than we need.

Step back.

Breathe.

Don't question why me? for to do this instils a victim mentality.

You are now a victim.

You chose for these events to happen.
For you to grow and expand your mind.
You may not realise now but you are breaking a cycle.
A cycle of hurt and pain.
It ends with you.

~~⊙~~

18/06/2019

Your World. Your Planet. Your Time
Look after what you already have.
There is far too much 'stuff' in this world
More than you can consume in your lifetime
Your children's lifetime
Reuse.
Get crafty and creative.
What can one object be used for in a different way?
Every year you buy.
Let's borrow and share, especially those items used once or twice a year.

~~⊙~~

01/07/2019

Do you ever feel as if you're swimming along with the tide?
You get up?
Go to work with the others?
Walk together.
Sit in an office for 8 or 9 hours wishing the clock would go faster.
Walking out.
Fall asleep on the bus or the tube.

Get home.

Make dinner.

Switch TV on.

Fall asleep.

Do it all again tomorrow.

And the next.

And the next.

Until it's Friday.

Yay Friday.

Two whole days to do what you want.

Two days.

Seven days in a week and you choose what you want to do in two days.

Hold on.

Whose life is this?

Is it yours?

Or your employers?

If you don't want to work 9–5 in an office job you don't have to.

You have a choice.

Create work you want to do.

Life is for living.

Not churning through.

Reach out and explore.

What fun could you have?

What would you enjoy doing?

Do it.

Ah but my mortgage/rent is too high.

You can choose to move.

Find what you enjoy

05/07/2019

We come through.

To guide you.

To show you a way.

To inhabit and live together on your planet.

To corroborate and collaborate.

Feeling a sense of community through action and joining in.

Through allowing space for yourself and others to create consciously and collectively.

To allow your creativity to flow.

To show up and demand for yourself the life you know you deserve.

Show up for you and others.

Demand for you and others.

Working together as a collective is multiple times more powerful than going alone.

Dream big.

What idea do you want to turn it into a reality?

Enjoy being you.

08/07/2019

Your time is best spent in meditation.

Dream.

Allow yourself to not do anything.

Space is required to expand.

Push beyond your current existing boundaries.

Dare to dream big.

To go where you haven't been before.

Beyond this space.

This life.

Progress and expand.

We need you to think bigger.

To expand your consciousness.

You already believe in you.

Believe more.

We want you to achieve your life purpose.

We want you to help others on a global scale.

Don't worry about the how.

Trust that we will put the right people and situations in front of you.

Keep taking note of the signs and symbols we are presenting to you.

Connection. Authenticity.

You are doing it your way. Non-conformist.

Allowing. Asking. Achieving. Creating.

The next 3 months will see big changes.

You have already mentioned that this is a pivotal time for many.

And you are correct.

There are huge transformations going on for many.

Not just you.

Changes in their thinking and beliefs.

Changes in their work.

Relationships.

Some will accept and roll with it.

Some may be confused by it.

You have been there.

You have found tools to be of use to others.
They may not realise it is a spiritual awakening.
It is.
Support and guide others on their journey.
Prepare them.
We don't want anyone to be scared.

~⌒~

1/08/2019

The portal has opened. It is time. TO step up and move forward. TO be bold and brave. It is no coincidence that the New Moon is in Leo and that we call the gateway the Lion gateway. For they both embrace the Lion qualities you see. The strength. The roar. We want to hear your loudest roar. Be proud of who you are. Be bold. Be brave. Be you. That is the sign Lindsay has in her house and it's true. We want you to embrace this time. Do something you wouldn't normally do. Now is not the time to have fear, oh no. Now is the time to go. What is the Lion gateway? Figuratively it is a portal. An area where we go between. It has been difficult at times for us to convey our messages as there has been a density of energy. Some of you don't believe we exist. Some of you have had a lot of work to do on yourself before you could begin to remember. To remember you and where you originated from. It has taken a little while longer than we had originally hoped but we are here now and finding it much easier to communicate with those of you who will or can take the time to listen. There is a reason we encourage meditation and yoga. It is so you become a clearer channel to listen to the signs we send. To listen to the world around you. To feel your energy being. TO feel your energy flowing. When your energy flows clear, like clean water, there is more fluidity. Embrace your clear channels, energetically. We will meet at the Lion Gateway. Ascend forwards. Into time and space. Into the higher realms as a higher being. When I begin to think is when I begin to lose my way. When I begin to feel is when I begin to find myself.

08/08/2019

The Lion Gates Portal. Ascend dear ones.
There is heightened activity in the skies that you may not be aware of.
This peak of energy will affect many of you in different ways.
Be kind to yourself and show yourself love.
Centre and protect your energies.

23/09/2019

Ah dear loved ones
As time moves on, we are getting closer
Closer to our new ways of living
Spiralling and ascending
Towards light and love
For those of you already practising keep forth and continue
For soon you will be in huge demand
Your services will be needed
Whilst anxiety and stress amplify
During times of uncertainty and crisis
You stand together
Come as one
Shine your light

Step into your power
Of being the light

It is time to unite
To move forward together

16/10/2019

We would like to remind you to be kind
To yourself, to others
Being kind doesn't take much energy
It can be a smile, a compliment, a simple hello
To a stranger

Kindness is infectious. It carries on and on and on and on
and on and on and on and on and on and On and on and on
and on and on and on and on and on and on and on and on
and on and on and on

You get the idea

Often you may find being kind to yourself
More difficult than to others
Your mind talks to you in a way that
May at times
Be detrimental to you
Be harsh to you
Be unkind to you
Your mind is a very powerful tool
It absorbs 'stuff' from others, their own thoughts
And opinions
Which can weigh you down
It is time to do some reverse engineering
For every time you have a negative thought, think of one

positive
Write a reminder, a post it
Eventually the positives will outweigh
The negatives
Be kind to others, Be kind to you

14/01/2020

We come through as messengers
Of light
Our connections are increasing
And more of you are able to
Hear us
For some of you, you can speak our thoughts
For some of you, you write our thoughts
For some of you, without even knowing how or why you are
Saying something, you are speaking
On our behalf
For the messages of love and light
Grow strong
My friend
The more we share
The stronger it becomes
There has been mention of a
World War
And this is true.
There is a wat
Between darkness and light
As we told you last year

There must be a breaking down
Of the old

In order to provide a New Earth
A new structure that works
For the many and not the few
It may seem scary, unnatural
Not the order of things
But it is a necessary turn for
All, for human consciousness and
The human race
Trust in the process xx

20/01/2020

When I was young
There were places I wanted to visit
Places unknown
Places hidden
Places beyond
I wanted to visit
I knew
In this time and space, it wasn't possible
However, upon closing my eyes
I journeyed
I visited places
Unbeknown to me
And many others
Places and spaces
Sacred

From the past I have been

And ventured

And seen

Where history has occurred

I left my energy

In this space

I left my heart

There

Expansive and conscious

For the future

For when others visit

They will feel it too

Honour our land

24/01/2020

How do we become comfortable with uncomfortable feelings?

Anger, Rage, Jealousy, Greed, Lust

WE deny them

We don't own them

Not part of me, we say

How can we be spiritual and loving?

Yet feel anger

How can we be awakened and kind?

Yet feel rage

How can we be compassionate and caring?

Yet feel greed

Owning all parts of ourselves

The whole

The parts perceived to be good
And not so good
They are all a part of you
And your wholeness
The more aware we become
Of the darker side, the shadow
The more light we shine on it
The anger and rage dissipate
The jealousy lessens
The greed subsides
Still there but not as prominent
Allow these feelings to arise
To transmute
To heal
To deal with
Some of us may have held onto
These feelings for years
Constantly ignoring them
Not listening
Then we hear a whisper
Something is stirred within us
What is it?
At the depth of my soul
What is it that wants to be acknowledged?
For acknowledging it is the initial step
Be aware it may feel uncomfortable
With these uncomfortable feelings
Is also part of the process
The process of growth

The process of learning

The process of becoming more you

⌒

04/02/2020

When you set your intentions from a place of love and for the greater good of all you are more likely to receive and achieve it.

Live from a place of love.

Believe from a place of love.

Love is central to all we do and feel and be.

Love has such a high vibration that it draws in opportunities and things you are desiring.

What do you desire?

⌒

10/02/2020

Creative expression

From a place of love

Following your heart, your dreams

Allowing your heart to lead the way

Rather than your head

Do what you love

Dance, sing, express yourself through

Movement

Be what you love

What does it look like?

What if you could be who you?

Wanted?

What would that look like?

Be expression

Be love

18/02/2020

Space in a relationship is of utmost paramountal importance

When we recognise that firstly as a person, we require space

Then can tell those we love we need space

Then can accept the time we have to ourselves without feeling guilt or shame

Then we have mastered the art of space

We do not always require the presence of another to fulfil our needs

We do not always require to depend on someone to fulfil our needs

We fulfil our own needs

We fulfil our own wants

We fulfil our own desires

And then we can look to another

To coexist alongside us

On our path

To cocreate alongside us

On our path

To be in our space, to be aware of our space, to be aware of their space

Transcending doubts and fears

Transcending the illusions in place

20/02/2020

Rest, dear ones, rest
Since the beginning of the year you have
Been catapulted
Into a state of productivity
There has been much energy pushing you forward
New ideas, new projects, old projects and completion
Today, breathe
Give yourself breathing space and time away
From the constant
What is it you LOVE to do?
For the more you do what you LOVE
The more that will come to you
This is how it works but this is a time to rest
Do what needs to be done
But what wants to be done can wait
The time restrictions we place on ourselves
Are illusions of time
Time is infinite
Yet we often hear people saying
We have no time
Prioritise your time
Choose how you spend it and
Who you spend it with
When you choose HOW you spend your time
It brings with it FREEDOM

27/02/2020

We all have our abilities and knowledge and utilise these in the best way we can to serve others and our space.

I'm not going to say much about the space yet as it is not the right time but I will.

We are aware of the work many of you are doing on the planet right now to raise the vibration of all and the collective consciousness.

Keep going.

It is the time to do this.

We are working with you as we are also aware that any shifts may affect our lives now.

Listen for signs, observe and follow them.

Trust what your heart says and follow that as opposed to the mind for too long the mind has won, governed, led.

It is time for the heart to lead.

Heart centred focus on relationships, work, family.

Love.

Love with all of your heart and every inch of your being.

Create the love you need for you and allow it to radiate out.

We are working with you.

01/03/2020

Often in times of rest we find the most clarity.

Allow yourself to truly rest and relax.

Your version of time is different to ours.

I know you have had several conversations recently that time is an illusion and it is.

We love that your kitchen clock is wrong and you changed the time on your car so you had no concept of time.

Our past, present and future all mingle together.
Sit and enjoy this time of rest.
Of contemplation for it will reap great rewards.

⌐◡

13/03/2020

Appearances can be deceptive
There is no doubt that this is a virus
Not seen before
And this is causing panic
Senses of feeling out of control
What we feel secure about is shifting
We did tell you this last year
That the systems would collapse
They have to, as to continue would bring the world to an end
What tools do you have at your disposal now to help you through this time?
Mindfulness- Fear not the Unknown
Gratitude
Looking after your physical body- eating fresh fruit and veg
How can you relax?
If your work is affected maybe there is an opportunity to retrain or start your own business?
If you are a healer or therapist it is time to stand in your power and shine your light
Continue to send messages of love to people on Facebook/ Instagram and Twitter. Send healing.

⌐◡

19/03/2020

Whilst some of us are stirred into action
Some of us may merely observe
The doers and the seers
Are of equal importance at this time
To get stuck in
To take action
To rouse and rally the troops
Doers are needed
The seers stand back
To observe
To view
From a higher perspective
The goings on around
What is needed afterwards
Post what feels like a crazy time
What do we want from our ideal world?
For many years, many have complained
About the life, about the stress
We don't want to live like this
The opportunity has arisen
To start again
To start afresh
The doers and the seers
Are of equal and utmost importance

20/03/2020

A Human Being Mandate

You are here to learn self-love, compassion, empathy and kindness

You will experience periods of low in order to experience periods of highs

Learn from every relationship

As we learn from abuse and heal ourselves, we break the chains of abuse.

Many of us have left abusive relationships to move forward into conscious relationships.

These are the future.

Role models of what a 'good' relationship looks like

⌒

20/03/2020

Day 1 of spring

New seeds are being planted

Literally and figuratively

When life becomes

A different experience to which we

Are accustomed

It opens our minds

To an awareness of possibilities

Which were previously hidden

Unearthed

Waiting for that tiny glimpse of light

Encouragement

To grow, to be

⌒

22/03/2020

The world isn't going to return
To the way it was before
We are currently in no man's land
Transitioning between the old and the new
Feeling our way through the darkness
Towards an unknown light
Working through the fear and worry

We will emerge individually and collectively
Different
In a good way
A returning to our souls knowing
Of the reasons for our being
We all chose to be here at this time
To transition and to emerge
As a new being

⌒

23/03/2020

Love in the time of Corona
If ever there was a time
To contemplate the grandeur of love
It is now
For with the feeling of fear that
Is amassed within the heart
The opposite feeling is love
For some, it starts as a crack
Releasing the hardening, the fissures
Creating a fracture

To allow the love slowly in
And out
It is always easier to see the love
We have for others
To go deep within
To love ourselves
And to love others unconditionally
Is the true meaning of love

⁓

25/03/2020

There is a tendency
For one
To get lost
Within their own thoughts
In their own world
Where their own problems are of utmost paramount
Importance
When a tragedy occurs
Or a pandemic
As you are currently seeing
One's own problems and concerns
Are put into perspective
When thoughts of others
Spring to mind
Before their own
Enhancing connection and compassion
To those fellow humans

⁓

About the Author

Lindsay Banks is a Spiritual Entrepreneur and Teacher. Having gone through her first spiritual awakening back in 2017 her spiritual journey continues. Learning to trust in the Universe/Upstairs/Source has allowed Lindsay to be guided along her path. Lindsay teaches spiritual development courses, empowering and facilitating healing for others on their journey. An advocate for Speaking Your Truth, Lindsay shares her own trials and tribulations of life and how you can work through them. A channeller for the Pleiadeans, spirits and past leaders Lindsay shares the messages that come through on her YouTube channel. Her programme The Spiritual Journey sees her interviewing others walking the spiritual path and how they are now helping others.

To find out more about Lindsay you can head to her website
www.lindsaybanks.uk

You can also find her on social media at

www.facebook.com/Lindsaybanks111

www.instagram.com/Lindsaybanks111

www.twitter.com/Lindsaybanks111

www.youtube.com/Lindsaybanks

You can also join Lindsay's free Facebook group,
Consciousness Arising

Resources

I am so grateful to everyone I meet along my path. Everyone helps me through their words and actions but I wanted to mention a few people I have mentioned in the book here for you to connect with if you feel drawn to

Lizi Walker- E.J Healing on Facebook

Daniela Pala- mystillpoint.co.uk

Katharine Lucy Haworth- OrangeBlossomWays

Viv Chamberlinn Kidd- www.essentiallyshamanic.co.uk

Dale Tobin- The Healing Path on Facebook

Maureen Wycherley- Joyous Living

June Tranmer- Wellbeing in York

David Sear- Hypnotherapy www.davidsear.co.uk

Leanne Juliette- Shamanic Priestess
    www.leannejuliette.com

Jote Prakash Singh- Kundalini Yoga teacher on Facebook

Books

Bringers of the Dawn- Barbara Marciniak

Shakti Woman- Vicki Noble

Return of the Bird Tribe- Ken Carey

Awakening- Pir Vilayat Inayat Khan

Women of Lemuria- Monika Muranyi

Guardians of Lemuria- Sarah Jane Ross

You are a Goddess- Sophie Bashford

Shamanism Made Easy- Christa Mackinnon

If Women Rose Rooted- Sharon Blackie